The Soul Cave

The Soul Cave

It's Never Too Late To Find Your Power

SANDRA FRANCIS

A record of this publication is available from the British Library.

ISBN 978-1-910027-57-8

Typesetting by Wordzworth Ltd
www.wordzworth.com

Cover design by Titanium Design Ltd
www.titaniumdesign.co.uk

Cover image by courtesy of Nika Tchokhonelidze

Published by Local Legend
https://local-legend.co.uk

This book is dedicated to my beautiful family,
on both sides of life, without whom
my life would lack so much.
Thank you so much for your endless support,
encouragement and unconditional love.

Acknowledgements

It's been eighteen months since I wrote the first words to the publication of *The Soul Cave*, and the book is very different to that early manuscript. I owe gratitude to so many people for supporting me through its development.

Firstly, I thank my teachers and mentors, Alison Wynne-Ryder and Pamela Goodall, for guiding me on my spiritual journey and for their friendship and wisdom that continues to inspire me. My good friend Glenys Stephenson has also been a constant support and a reliable sounding board, keeping me sane.

I am grateful to my late husband for teaching me the soul lessons I needed to learn in this life, enabling me to understand how to let go of the past, and to my family for their support, honesty and grounding.

Finally, I thank Nigel Peace, owner of Local Legend. This book is far better than I could have hoped, thanks to his encouragement, knowledge and endless patience.

https://local-legend.co.uk

About the Author

Sandra is a writer, psychic, clairvoyant medium and healer. She came to spirituality "by accident" in middle age after attending a meditation class, to find peace during a challenging time in her life, and finding herself immediately at home with all things psychic. Development courses and the guidance of significant spiritual mentors followed.

Living with an autoimmune condition, Sandra moved from the UK to Spain with her late husband for the benefits of the climate, and has taken on a new lease of life there with "no intention of growing old gracefully".

She runs websites for local information and spirituality, works as a freelance writer and editor for clients around the world, and offers spiritual guidance, crystal therapy, energy healing and readings locally and online.

https://sandrassoulcave.com/

Disclaimer

All the accounts described in this book are true. However, the names and other identifying features of people mentioned have been changed to protect their privacy.

Contents

Introduction

There are times when we all feel the need to make better sense of what is going on in our lives. Perhaps we believe that we've already dealt with the problems and traumas of the past, yet still find it difficult to forgive, to leave the past behind and move forward. Or maybe we are simply convinced that there are more dimensions to life than we can see right now, but we're not sure where to look for more insight and guidance…

It's time to find our own Soul Cave!

This is where we discover everything we need to make sense of our past and to look forward to a future where we create our reality rather than settling for whatever life throws at us.

Once upon a time, I had a room for psychic readings and spiritual healing that I called Sandra's Soul Cave, and this now lives on as a spiritual concept, the sacred space where I receive comfort, guidance and clarity on a regular basis. It's my own special haven where I access the wisdom of my higher self and call on the help and support of angels, spirit guides and ascended masters. Wherever I am, there is the Soul Cave, and when I work with clients I do my best to help them access their own sacred spaces and find the answers they need to guide them through the challenges and lessons of life.

I've found that many people can identify with this concept and I hope you will also be able to, finding something in these pages that resonates with you and inspires you to explore further. You don't need to believe in anything in particular to access your own Soul Cave, other than yourself.

Connecting with your Soul Cave means going deep within that self and uncovering layers of experience and understanding that may have lain hidden and undiscovered for many years, perhaps many lifetimes. It's a journey of adventure, rather like exploring real caves, but now it's the soul and its wisdom we're seeking. Our personal journeys are internal and spiritual, rather than external and physical, but they're just as demanding because during them we are all tested in so many ways.

Caves can be dark, complex and difficult to navigate, and although I intend this book to be healing and uplifting, as every spiritual book should be, there are inevitably some unsettling episodes to be described. There are some passages that are difficult to read, just as they have been difficult to write. However, there are always hidden treasures waiting for us to access them, and even the dark times can help to bring about illumination for the soul.

And I hope to show that it is never too late for us to step into our power and embrace our destiny, as I did in mid-life after many years of uncertainty. Moreover, I will show that we are never given greater challenges than we are able to deal with; we can work through the most difficult times and emerge stronger, with a renewed purpose and zest for life.

So come along with me to explore the Soul Cave.

CHAPTER ONE

Warnings From Spirit

It was a few minutes before midnight and I had been watching murder mysteries on TV with my husband, Ted. This would seem ironic later. After several episodes and a bottle of white wine, it was time to sleep and I made for the bedroom with my dog Paddy hot on my heels as usual, leaving Ted to lock up and follow us. That mundane ending to quite a pleasant evening signalled the end of Normal Life and the beginning of a Nightmare.

It was as though I had left Dr Jekyll and Mr Hyde had taken his place. The next thing I knew, Ted was shouting and pulling at Paddy, trying to get him off the bed as my normally laid-back hound bared his teeth in warning. The easy atmosphere of the evening had suddenly become very menacing. I reached out to soothe Paddy but he wrenched himself from my grasp and leapt after my husband. I followed as quickly as I could, only to find them both on the floor in the kitchen of our static caravan with Paddy's powerful jaws clamped around Ted's upper arm. Why was he behaving so out of character?

I grabbed my dog by the collar and he span round, biting the index finger of my left hand in his panic, but I was so intent on defusing the situation that I never even felt it. My whole focus was on safely resolving an incident that was rapidly escalating out of control.

Suddenly, Paddy gave the softest of whimpers and the light left his eyes. The last thing he saw in this world was not the rage clouding Ted's face but the love and grief in my own eyes as I had to say goodbye to my beautiful boy. For that small mercy, I am eternally grateful. Paddy was dead, but I couldn't work out how or why – until I noticed that my arm was covered in way too much blood to have come from my bitten finger.

Then I saw the blade, still clutched in Ted's right hand. He had killed my dog with a knife that he would admit, as we waited for the emergency services to arrive, had been intended for me. He'd suffered a deadly mood swing in the moments between my going into the bedroom and him locking up and following. And Paddy had given his life to protect me.

Paddy's death had been foretold, although I didn't realise it at that moment. Three weeks before, I'd had my first ever proper Tarot reading when the reader had spoken of "an accident in the kitchen" and warned me to be careful with my left hand. She also told me that I would return to Spain, where we had moved earlier for health reasons, but that Ted would not be with me, and she saw me with a different, female black and white dog.

As well as this information coming just days before that life-changing night, a friend in my spiritual circle warned me not to leave Paddy and Ted together. So the signs were there. Unfortunately, I wasn't able to interpret or believe them and save my dog's life.

Perhaps I wasn't meant to, though.

In the confusion of his last moments, Paddy bit through my left index finger to the bone, making quite a mess in the process. That finger is still a funny shape compared to the others but it works as well as ever. I know I am lucky to carry such small physical scars from that night. The resulting emotional scars are now also healed – and how that has been achieved is at the heart of this book – to the point where I can remember Ted with love and truly miss his presence. He passed to Spirit around a year after that night and we never spent another night under the same roof.

How did all of this come about? That cold night in the middle of March was the horrific finale to three years of mental and physical abuse brought about by cirrhosis of the liver, which had led to inflammation of Ted's brain, to paranoia and to psychosis. Often known as Wet Brain Syndrome, this is common in end-stage alcoholics and causes confusion, anger and personality changes. Because of Ted's advanced age, doctors had put his symptoms down to dementia and hadn't investigated further.

Perhaps the outcome would have been different if they had. What is certain, though, is that the effects of prolonged alcohol abuse on Ted's brain brought on a fatal mood swing that turned a pleasant evening into a scene from a horror movie. For the leading actors, life would never be the same again. And only one of us would get out of it alive.

Some time before these events, my friend Gill had come to Spain to spend Christmas and New Year with us and to celebrate her birthday. She noticed how verbally abusive and irrational Ted had become, and told me she didn't want to leave us alone as she feared he would become physically violent if she returned home. She ended up staying for six months. Her premonition proved to be right, because the attack came the first night we were alone together, having ourselves returned to England.

I left him of course, but it was clear that he was seriously ill and he begged me to take him back to Spain to die. I was torn in two as I wanted to do what was best for him, despite all that had happened. During our separation, I continued to take him shopping and to medical appointments; we were in regular contact, he seemed to be calmer and he wasn't as physically strong as he'd been before.

Besides, he was my husband and I still loved him. I'm sure many people will recognise that our default setting when we love someone deeply is to be there for our partners through the bad times, in the hope and belief that we can go on to enjoy more good times together.

And I hadn't always had to tread on eggshells around Ted, it wasn't his nature to be violent towards me or any other living creature. Until illness turned him into a stranger to be feared, he was the most exciting man I had ever met, even though he was several years older than me. During almost three decades together, we made some wonderful memories and he was a supportive husband as well as my best friend.

But we never know what's around the corner or how things can change in an instant, perhaps just as well for the sake of our sanity. And sometimes, the strongest and best thing we can do is to recognise when we have done everything in our power and to walk away while we still can. Paddy's death eventually made me see there was nothing more I could do for Ted, no matter how much my instinct was to nurse and support him through his final months.

In the end, it seemed to come down to him or me and I had to choose me, because anything else would have been a blatant disregard for Paddy's heroic actions and his ultimate sacrifice. I owed it to Paddy's memory, not only to find a way to live in peace and happiness but to make sense of what had just happened, and use the resulting insights to help others going through tough challenges.

Otherwise, what was it all for?

I'm sorry that this part of my story may have been difficult to read, even harrowing, but there is an essential point to it, which is to show that it is possible to emerge from even the worst traumas feeling stronger, with a deeper sense of peace and a renewed zest for life.

Effectively, I also lost my husband on the night Paddy died. Of course, I am not the first to deal with devastating loss and I certainly won't be the last. However, I do believe that everything happens for a reason, and that's why I am sharing my subsequent discoveries and beliefs and describing how I was able to process the events of that night and the previous years, make sense of them and make a new start after hitting the lowest point in life. I did it with the help of friends, family and the spirit worlds, and I hope that something here will resonate and help you navigate through and heal from your own traumas, whatever form they may take.

> At the end of the day, all we can do is try to learn from
> our experiences, both good and bad, and refuse to allow
> the events of the past to define and direct our future.

It may not always seem like it, but we are never alone with our challenges. I have come to believe that Spirit always has our backs, and that we receive signs and signals to help us make our best choices. We may not always recognise spirit warning signs for what they are at the time but, when we reflect on events later, they can help us to strengthen our psychic connections, develop our intuition and emerge stronger and happier from even the most challenging experiences.

Have you ever been planning to do something, then changed your mind at the last minute? Maybe you have had a bad feeling about someone or something and cancelled an arrangement or perhaps travelled on a different train than you had intended to take. There didn't seem to be a single good reason to make the switch, but a gut feeling told you to change your plans.

We usually call this intuition, especially if it later transpires that it was the right thing to do. Perhaps nothing dramatic happened as a result – or we're not aware of any such event – but often, when we look back on these moments, we just know we made the right call by changing our plans at the last minute. It may well be that Spirit is warning us away from potential problems, or guiding us towards something or someone better.

Indeed, whenever we decide to do something that we can't justify with logic, I believe it's likely to be the result of a sign from Spirit. This could either be highlighting an inconsistency in our thinking or behaviour that we need to be aware of or encouragement that things are moving forward as planned. A sequence of spiritual signs can indicate that the timing is wrong and our plans need tweaking, or confirm that now is the ideal time. Either way, we should learn to pay attention to such signs and consider their meanings carefully.

As our spiritual connections strengthen, we pick up on more and more signs of guidance around all sorts of situations, both positive and negative. By opening our hearts and minds to spiritual guidance we can receive valuable information to help us navigate safely through our challenges. We may not immediately recognise these occurrences for what they are but, when we find time for reflection, we are invariably able to see the bigger picture and process our feelings around situations and events. This can be invaluable when dealing with past troubles, allowing us to move forward with our lives.

Here's an unusual example of how spiritual guidance can reach us. A week before Paddy died, one of my most trusted spiritual mentors mentioned she was holding a full-day workshop about dragons, and I jumped at the chance to learn more about these beautiful creatures. They've had a bad press in history, yet many believe they have a loving and protective energy and are eager to help us spiritually if we allow them into our lives. Later, I would use a deck of dragon oracle cards for readings whenever I felt my client needed protection or the cleansing energy of the fire dragons.

Now, many will not share these beliefs, of course, and that's fine because we all have to find what works for us and where best we can gain the comfort, guidance, clarity and insights we seek. However, as I have learned more about dragon energy, whether that be real or symbolic, I have certainly come to believe in its ability to assist us spiritually if we want it to.

That workshop was certainly a revelation for me in more ways than one. During a meditation to meet our 'personal dragons', we were each encouraged to ask its name. Our teacher put forward the theory that different dragons come and go in our lives depending on the situations we are dealing with; today's dragon may not be the best fit to help with tomorrow's challenges. That made sense to me, at least, although I can see why it may not resonate with everyone. (But that's the wonderful thing about the way Spirit works: we can each choose what we want to place our faith in and there's no one-size-fits-all belief system that everyone has to get their heads around.)

The dragon that appeared in my meditation was a beautiful green colour, the same shade, as I had learned, as Archangel Raphael's emerald healing ray. To my astonishment, he gave his name as Paddy and said that his sole purpose in life was to protect me.

Later, as we shared our meditation experiences, the workshop leader explained that dragons are our protectors and they can take on many different forms or none. In other words, they may not actually look like dragons at all and could be embodied in other ways, or simply appear to us in thoughts and dreams. According to this idea, it seemed that my dog was also my dragon!

Thinking about this later, it made perfect sense to me. Paddy was very much my dog and had always been protective of me. If we met someone we didn't know on our walks, Paddy would growl, warning them to keep their distance. To avoid this, I developed the habit of saying "Hello" to everyone who came towards us whether I knew them or not; it earned me a few funny looks but at least it kept Paddy's protective instincts in check and I made one or two lasting friendships as a result. More recently, whenever Ted had become angry with me for no good reason, Paddy would gently intervene to defuse the moment before it escalated, warning Ted to play nicely. My dog had always been my protector and now, it seemed, he was also my very own dragon.

A few days later, at my weekly psychic development circle, the friend mentioned earlier asked where Paddy was and warned me not to leave him alone with Ted, since she could see pain around them. As it happened, Paddy was staying at a friend's house, with his canine friend Gizmo for company while we attended circle. (These two were the archetypal Odd Couple, Paddy being a mix of Great Dane and Labrador weighing thirty-five kilos, compared to Gizmo's four kilos of Chihuahua-Papillon cross. They were the best of friends although it was Gizmo who ruled the roost.)

I was startled by this warning but I took on board what she said, trusting her intuition and promising not to leave Paddy alone with Ted even for a short time. It would mean some creative thinking around my usual routine but, if Spirit were sending me a warning, I wanted to listen. Tragically, I never got to put my plans into action because just two days later Paddy was dead and Ted needed two operations to repair the damage to his right arm.

True, my dog and my husband were not technically alone together when Paddy died, but I was not in the room with them so my friend's prediction was verified. My dog died protecting me and he was also the dragon who courageously came to the aid of the damsel in distress. And the whole thing had also been foretold in my Tarot reading. The spiritual signs and guidance around the situation were nothing short of amazing.

When everything was new and raw, I was angry about these warnings because I felt that surely they should have helped to prevent Paddy's death. Once I began to come to terms with what happened, though, I could draw some comfort from the experience. Importantly, it proved that any concerns about my husband's behaviour were spot on, because Spirit could see the bigger picture and knew something was badly wrong. That recognition alone validated my intuition and, when you are processing trauma and blaming yourself for not doing things differently, validation matters a lot. I could at least trust my instincts, although sadly I wasn't able to influence the outcome because that was a consequence of another's choices.

Naturally, we often wonder how we can be sure that the signs or warnings from Spirit are exactly that and not merely our own wishful thinking or self-fulfilling prophesies, our own negativity bringing about the things we are so anxious to avoid. Well, it seems to me that when the guidance is voiced by others who know little about us or our personal situation, that's a pretty clear indication of Spirit at work, especially when there are such specific insights as in my story.

But we can also encourage this guidance ourselves. When we are deep in meditation our mind is still, especially if it's a guided meditation and we are concentrating on the voice of a teacher. We will often be surprised by the things that come through in meditation because it can be stuff we would never expect to hear in a million years. (My dog being my dragon is a prime example.) Have you ever had something significant just pop into your head out of nowhere? If you have, this could be a spiritual sign so it should be welcomed and acted upon because it's likely to be something you really need to know rather than what you may like to hear.

We may also receive signs from loved ones in the afterlife, letting us know they are here with a message for us; again, we wonder how we can be sure that what we are being given is a true spiritual sign. In the next chapter, I shall describe a spirit visit from my mother and father. How did I know it was them, especially as I didn't see them? Mainly, I could tell by their personal energy. The more we work with energy, the more we are able to distinguish between different kinds: angels seem to have a totally different energy to loved ones in spirit, and the dragons I love to work with have yet another energy, more passionate and playful.

Of course, these are just my experiences and yours may be totally different, should you decide you want to work with Spirit. The path in life is an individual experience and what works for one may not resonate with another. I only hope that something here will ignite a spark and you will wish to investigate further; the more we learn the more empowered we become, and there's always the chance that we will make one or two life-changing discoveries! Sometimes it will be a case of just 'knowing' who or what we're working with without actually knowing how we know.

And if we're unsure, we should not be too shy to ask for guidance or confirmation. Indeed, very often we develop a 'personal signal' from Spirit: mine is a burning in my left ear, as though someone has just struck a match close by. That's my signal that I'm on the right course and it's great confirmation when it comes, if a little uncomfortable for a few moments!

Those in the spirit worlds will always find a way to let us know they are with us, and we come to recognise the personal signs. We may experience physical sensations such as the example above or maybe a tightening in the chest when someone is around who passed from a heart attack. When our instinct recognises this as a sign of spirit presence, we need to acknowledge it and simply ask them to take any pain or breathlessness away.

But it's also possible to feel physical sensations such as chest pain, nausea or palpitations, around people who may not have our best interests at heart. Daisy, a friend's teenage daughter, often felt nauseous around her boyfriend but was then always fine once she was back home. She had no problems around anyone else and no other symptoms. She began to work out that maybe something was wrong in their relationship, so it wasn't entirely unexpected when one of her friends said she'd seen him out with another girl and a baby, apparently very close. Of course, the boyfriend hadn't said anything about the other girl and the baby, who turned out to be his child, so this was a red flag. Clearly, the nausea had been a sign that things weren't as they seemed and she hasn't experienced it since.

Another way that Spirit may send signs for us is through random meetings. A friend of mine, Sarah, told me she was interested in dating a mutual friend, Ron, but couldn't be sure if he felt the same, even though people who knew them said it was obvious he liked her. She was a widow and ready for another relationship, but didn't want to risk spoiling their friendship by making the wrong assumptions. I suggested she ask Spirit for a sign.

A few days later, we were both at our busy local market and, as we turned the corner into another aisle, there was Ron. Sarah still wasn't convinced but agreed that if there were more signs she wouldn't ignore them. A few days later, she was in a large supermarket several miles away and there he was again, blocking her access to the cherry tomatoes. That same evening, she was out with friends for a meal and, sure enough, there was Ron in the same restaurant, dining with his friends.

None of these meetings happened near to where we all lived, so both Sarah and Ron came to believe they were being brought together. They are both rather shy but the chance meetings broke the ice and soon they started dating regularly. Was it just coincidence? Whenever they were out and about locally they hardly ever met by chance, yet once Sarah asked for a sign they came in thick and fast. And signs, once we recognise them as such, encourage us to take notice, make connections and start to think about things differently.

So-called coincidences may often be signs from Spirit that something should happen, or should not. Indeed, I no longer believe in coincidence and nor do most of the spiritual people I know; when they are so meaningful they are genuine synchronicities.

My reading and treatment room, Sandra's Soul Cave, was originally a room that I had chosen in a friend's suite of offices, basically just four walls, a floor and a ceiling. Although I really wanted it, I wondered whether I could afford the rent as well as the fixtures and fittings to furnish it. I had a figure in mind for the rent, and that was the exact amount my friend asked for. The first sign.

Now, how was I going to furnish it? I was having work done in my garden at the time and the builder had just acquired an office for his business and wanted to get rid of the existing furniture: club chairs, dining chairs, a table and a glass display cabinet (ideal for crystals!). He didn't want anything for it, just wanted it all out of the way. The second sign. Now I needed a lamp for a more gentle light, as the room's main lighting was too harsh. Next day, what was left outside by the bins but a perfectly good, working standard lamp with a lovely gentle light. This was the third sign in two days and now I had my Soul Cave.

These were important first steps on my spiritual journey. Through having a physical presence in my small hometown, I made a lot of useful connections which may have taken years to gather otherwise and I became better known. So if we are presented with an opportunity, and feel that it's right for us but we are hesitating to commit, we should ask for a sign from Spirit, then be ready for it. We never know where it may lead us.

As mentioned, Spirit may even use a 'calling card' to get our attention, like the burning near my ear. When I used to attend a development circle at a friend's home in Plymouth, my father would often come along and announce himself to me with the pungent aroma of the Senior Service cigarettes he had smoked. I was just sixteen when he passed and I haven't been around anyone who smokes them since then, yet I still recognise the familiar smell. The circle leader also sensed his presence and remarked that she had never smelled tobacco like that, even though her own father had also smoked and she often smelled his personal tobacco in her apartment. In life, my Dad would always place a gentle hand on my left shoulder when he wanted to attract my attention from behind, rather than calling out to me, and he still does that every time he comes through.

Coming to recognise and accept the spiritual signs during the three weeks prior to Paddy's death would play a big part in helping me heal from the trauma of that night. But in the immediate fallout I needed to find a way to forgive the seemingly unforgiveable. And I would have to do it alone, because after that night I could no longer live under the same roof as my partner of thirty years. There was no guarantee that there wouldn't be another, similar episode and who would protect me now that my canine dragon, my guardian angel with a waggy tail, was no longer here for me?

CHAPTER TWO

Forgiving the Unforgiveable

Have you ever been in a situation where something awful has happened, and you know it's not your doing, in fact you've done everything you could think of to avoid it? Perhaps you just knew that something bad was brewing, even though you didn't know just what it was, and you were powerless to avoid it. In the aftermath of such situations there's always such a mix of negative emotions: anger, recrimination, blame, guilt or even hatred. We may feel we will never be able to forgive the perpetrators and our lives will never be the same again because, very often, the ones who hurt us most are the ones we have trusted the most.

Can we ever recover from this and enjoy life again? Yes, because we're stronger than we know. In the meantime, though, how do we even begin to shift away from the negativity of the situation and let go of the past? The ability to forgive has helped some people I know to move on, whilst one other, sadly, has not been able to do so.

Margaret is a very spiritual person in many ways but she feels that she is up against a block when it comes to forgiving her late mother for her behaviour towards her. They never formed a truly loving bond and, although Margaret tried many times to reach out to her mother and look after her in later life, when she eventually passed there was a lot of unresolved anger as well as grief to deal with.

Several people have tried to help Margaret resolve this but she insists that she can never forgive her mother. Each time this happens, she will recount an instance of just why forgiveness is impossible. Of course, she then relives the experience and all the emotions she had experienced at the time come back to her. The effect is like having a dressing on a wound and then ripping it off rather than gently removing it. Any healing that's happened due to treatment with lotions, antibiotics or painkillers is then negated by not acknowledging the need for care, and the wound starts to hurt all over again. This time, though, the pain is worse because you thought you were on the road to recovery and now you realise there is still a very long way to go.

In Margaret's case, her caring friends and her spiritual practices do bring happiness and comfort into her life, which softens the edges of her trauma. However, because she is still unwilling to forgive, she is in a constant cycle of reopening old wounds and feeling the pain anew. Until she realises this, the situation is unlikely to change so one can only hope that she will come to see that forgiveness is the best gift she can give herself. Although Margaret has people around her who are willing to help her heal, she must make the decision herself.

Another friend also experienced a fraught mother-daughter relationship. Grace described her daughter as "an attention-seeker with no self-awareness", and even studying for a Psychology degree had not brought about changes in attitude. On the other hand, Ruby blamed her issues on her mother not being around enough when she was a child due to her demanding job in the medical profession. Yet there was no shortage of love there and Grace's son, Harry, had a totally different recollection of their childhood, saying that, although their parents didn't have much free time, they made sure to do things together as a family. He really couldn't see what the problem was.

But life for Grace was very stressful since she never knew what to expect when Ruby visited. All was well one moment, then something would trigger Ruby and she would subject her mother to a forensic description of her failings, followed by a dramatic exit and lengthy, recriminatory text messages. Then everything would go quiet until a few days later when Ruby would show up again as if nothing had happened.

I met Grace at a meditation group and we bonded straight away as she gradually told me her story. I was drawn to her because she looked on edge and I really wanted her to relax and enjoy the group, but she found it difficult to settle into the meditations well. After a couple of weeks, the group leader planned a forgiveness meditation and we spent some time talking about what we needed to forgive and how we felt our lives would improve if we could do that. Grace opened up about the situation with her daughter. She said she was spending more and more time away from home because that was the only way she could be sure Ruby wouldn't show up and turn everything upside down again, although she was annoyed with herself for feeling that way.

During the meditation, we were guided first to acknowledge anything in our perception that may be leading us to judge those we needed to forgive. Then we should recognise that we are not responsible for how other people behave and think, so we should not blame ourselves for what happens. Grace would later tell me that this awareness was now engraved in her soul. In that group, Grace came to understand why she felt as she did and gained an insight into Ruby's perceptions. She was now much calmer about the situation and was able to take Ruby's outbursts in her stride. As a bonus, because Grace was more relaxed, Ruby became less volatile and life was much more serene.

Pauline went through the trauma of rape and a resulting pregnancy as a teenager. Then, when the child was born it was discovered that Pauline had a rare and asymptomatic gynaecological condition that could have killed her at any time: it was a ticking time bomb, waiting to detonate. Back then, Pauline had cursed her luck that not only was she a parent before she was emotionally and practically ready, through no fault of her own, she also had to endure and recover from major surgery.

Over the following years, she married three times with each union ending in divorce. Whilst she acknowledged that responsibility for the break-ups was shared, she felt that the unresolved issues relating to the rape and the birth of her child had contributed significantly to her situation. She even blamed herself for the rape, and then for not being strong enough to put it behind her and move forward. Pauline turned to spirituality to find the answers she needed and, when she began to consider the concept of forgiveness, she realised that there are many different layers involved.

Pauline decided that not only did she need to forgive her rapist, she owed him gratitude for saving her life, because that early pregnancy meant her medical condition was resolved before it got to the stage where it could prove fatal. Once she had acknowledged this and sent forgiveness together with gratitude to the person, she immediately felt lighter and happier than she had in many years. She said that she felt as though she was truly living now rather than just coping and surviving, and her life was so much more enjoyable. Despite saying "Never again" after her third divorce, she felt ready to open her heart to love again.

True forgiveness is a powerful and empowering thing, helping us to let go of the past and move on. And whilst letting go and forgiveness work closely together, there are subtle differences between the two. We may be able to let go of the anger and frustration about a situation without actually forgiving those responsible for it; that may be enough, depending on how badly we were affected by it. However, if a certain person fills our heart and mind with negative emotions because of their words or actions, then maybe only forgiveness will do.

Letting go is probably easier to achieve, by acknowledging feelings and situations then looking at them in a different way. For example, suppose we felt unfairly treated when we lost the job we loved, although nobody in particular was responsible. Let's examine those feelings of unfairness and ask why they bother us. If it's the fact that we are now out of work, well, unfortunately that's a fact of life and there's nothing to be done about it.

But feeling like we shouldn't have been made redundant, for example, is more or less saying that somebody else should have lost their job instead. Is that how we really feel? Perhaps we just need to accept that it happened and nobody is to blame. That's letting go. However, if the reality is different and we feel that we lost our job as a result of someone else's actions, then we may need to forgive them before we can move on.

We can always choose how to react to such situations. When we decide to forgive the person who has hurt us, we are giving ourselves the gift of peace of mind. That person might have done wrong, but planning revenge and letting anger consume us isn't going to change the situation and it isn't going to help us move forward. Anger may seem an internal emotion but it can also be sensed and seen by others, affecting all our relationships; it ties us to the past and prevents us from enjoying the present moment. It's difficult to think clearly and make plans when we are focused on the unfairness of life and the nastiness of others. Letting go and practising forgiveness returns our focus to where it's most needed.

I confess that I didn't find it easy at first. How could I move on from the trauma of seeing a much-loved pet killed in front of me as he tried to protect me? It was challenging to say the least, and in those awful early weeks my first instinct was to turn away from the spiritual path that had brought me so much comfort and peace during the years of living with Ted's illness. It seemed as though, while I was doing the inner work and striving to be the best version of myself, life just carried on regardless. The more I tried to live positively, the more negativity came my way.

Gradually, though, I began to process the warnings that had foreshadowed Paddy's passing and I came to see them as signposts to healing, valuable lessons that nothing is ever as it seems. It made me realise that sometimes we need to look hard and deeply in order to recognise the truth before us. There are countless situations where we may need to exercise forgiveness and I'm sure many readers are saying, "I can forgive, but I can never forget what happened." I've certainly said that myself a number of times over the years.

It was only when I began to learn more about how energy works that I finally realised that, once those words are uttered, any hopes of true forgiveness have left the building. If we accept that everything has energy, then every interaction we have, whether good or otherwise, is also energy; in turn, this means that remembering past hurts keeps us attached to the negative past situations and prevents us from moving forward with our lives and reclaiming our joy. Clearly, if something really bad has happened we are unlikely literally to forget all about it; but what we need to do is find a way to reduce its importance and effect on us. I believe true forgiveness can help us do that, and it certainly worked for me.

I now see the events leading up to Paddy's death through a different lens and understand more about myself and why I became so negative, as well as learning how to shift my energy to a more positive perspective. It hasn't been easy and it's an ongoing exercise that's now become a way of life. Our journey to forgiveness becomes possible when we stop apportioning blame, whether to ourselves or to others. It doesn't mean we have to condone the other's actions, nor does it make what they did right. But when we also realise that certain things happened just because things needed to change, and not because the universe has it in for us, we're well along the path of acceptance.

One of my spiritual mentors is big on forgiveness, calling it "a sacred gift to oneself". True forgiveness is liberating because it frees us from the energetic attachments of the past. Of course, it's not as easy as just telling someone you forgive them and leaving it at that, rather it's like removing layers from an onion. Each layer that peels away uncovers a different surface, which can bring further challenges, so forgiveness is something that needs to be practised often and from the heart. Yet it need not take a long time, and it can be done anywhere, provided we can focus both heart and mind on the matter in hand.

Moreover, our most testing times can also be ideal opportunities to learn essential lessons about ourselves and others if we are open to the possibility. When the dust settles, we can reflect on these experiences and re-evaluate our soul's journey, newly equipped with the life lessons we have recently assimilated. And the knowledge that Spirit knows what is coming also demonstrates, as in my story, that we aren't alone with our problems. Strange as it may seem, that realisation helped to restore my faith and allowed me to take those important initial steps on my own healing journey.

I have completely forgiven Ted now. I've also forgiven myself, for not reading the signs earlier and removing myself and Paddy from the dangerous environment. And I've forgiven Paddy too. If that sounds strange, imagine how I felt when it was first brought to my attention that my dog needed forgiveness. After all, he saved my life, didn't he, and heroes don't need forgiveness.

It came about like this. One day, around a month after Paddy died, I was heading into town on the bus when, without warning, a wave of anguish washed over me. Not wanting to get off the bus or break down in public, I took myself into meditation because that always helps and I'm fortunate to be able to go deep very quickly; I knew I could give my spirit the boost it needed without missing my stop. Also, I learned during my psychic development training to work closely with angel energy, so it seemed natural to invite them into such an important meditation. I asked Archangel Jeremiel, the angel of forgiveness, and Archangel Michael, angel of justice and protection, to be present and help me.

I felt their comforting presence around me as I inwardly stated my intention to forgive Ted and to forgive myself for my own role in the situation, and almost immediately I felt my grief begin to recede. But then I was jolted out of the meditation by a loud voice saying, "Don't forget to forgive Paddy as well." The voice was so real and so close that I looked around my fellow passengers, certain that one of them must have spoken to me and at the same time feeling foolish because I must have been talking out loud. However, everyone was going about their business, looking at their phones, talking to children or getting ready to alight at their stop. Nobody even looked my way so I knew the voice had been in my head and part of the meditation.

Clearly, I was overlooking a crucial part of the forgiveness process by not examining all aspects of the situation, and the angels were reminding me right there on the bus that day.

I had asked myself repeatedly why Paddy had to leave me like that. In the years since I rescued him, he had become my main support and comfort as Ted's condition deteriorated and I had relied on him, rather than my husband. And whilst I was eternally grateful to him for saving my life, the selfish part of me was furious with him for leaving me all alone.

So the problem was that while I was replaying all these negative thoughts I couldn't get on with my life. I was reliving that night constantly, hanging on to the past, and it was ruining the present and looking set to adversely influence the future too. I had to break that cycle and move forward, because I couldn't let one traumatic night define me: I decided then and there that I wasn't a victim, I was and will always be a survivor. Forgiving Paddy for leaving me was an essential link in the process.

I managed to complete my meditation session on the bus, during a journey lasting around twenty minutes, and I felt infinitely better for it. Whenever I have felt myself focusing on past events since then, I have repeated the exercise and believe that something like this could help anyone needing to forgive or to heal. (There are many 'Forgiveness Meditations' on the Internet to choose from – still the mind and see what you are drawn to – and alternatively I offer some simple visualisations in this book too.)

A year or so later, I found myself dealing with forgiveness from a very different angle. It was just an ordinary Tuesday afternoon when my friend Gill and I were watching a quiz on TV. She's been a big support to me for many years and has also done a lot of inner work. Like me, she turned to spirituality to cope with trauma in her life and also discovered that she was more connected than she could ever have believed possible.

On this particular afternoon, she was first to notice a difference in the atmosphere, a coldness in the room despite the heating being on. She said she thought Ted was here and wondered whether he'd now passed to Spirit. I already knew that this was possible because he'd suffered a stroke a few months earlier and his daughter had recently informed me that she didn't think he had long to live. I had asked if I could see him but she wouldn't allow it in case my visit upset him. Besides, the nursing home only allowed one visitor to be there at the time of passing and she'd decided that it would be her.

Given Gill's announcement and the feeling in the room, I asked Spirit for confirmation that Ted was indeed with us; I immediately felt the familiar burning in my left ear and knew for sure that my parents were with me. I believe Dad is my 'gate keeper' as he has been near me a lot in recent years. We had been very close and he'd come to me in a dream, accompanied by both my grandfathers, just a day or two after he passed. However, it was most unusual for Mum to appear with him as she did today. She has come to me in meditations and dreams, but usually as a supportive observer rather than a messenger or adviser.

This time, though, she explained why Ted, or rather his energy, was with us. He had not yet passed and was hanging on to life by a thread because he needed forgiveness from me for the way he had behaved over the last few years. My parents had brought him so I could assure him that he was forgiven and could pass peacefully to Spirit. I sent him love, as did Gill, and we impressed on him that he was indeed forgiven.

He wasn't convinced, though, because the next afternoon the three of them were back again. Mum explained that he didn't believe I could possibly have forgiven him, especially for Paddy's death. This was ironic, really. When I had started my psychic development course, he'd been quite dismissive of "that weird stuff", as he called it. Now he was finding out at first hand that, 'There are more things in Heaven and Earth… than are dreamt of in your philosophy.' (Hamlet: Act 1, Scene 5)

How was I so certain that it was my parents with me, and that it was indeed Ted's energy we felt at the time? As mentioned previously, Dad has his own particular calling cards, sometimes a waft of Senior Service and always the hand on my shoulder when he's around. As far as Mum's presence goes, I sense it's her energy because it's pretty much intertwined with Dad's; there was nobody he was so close to in life apart from me, so it makes sense that their energies are still very much linked on the other side of life. Moreover, when anyone in Spirit speaks to me, I hear their voice in my head.

When one hears a spirit voice there are the nuances of expressions and choice of words that we remember, especially with our loved ones. And we become familiar with an individual's personal energy; the more we practise, the more we fine tune our perception of different energies.

We could feel that Ted's energy was much weaker when he returned that following day, and we wondered how best to help him. It was clear we needed angelic help so we called on Archangel Michael. Angel 'purists' may say it should have been Jeremiel, the angel of forgiveness; but, when I need to act decisively and quickly, I choose what is most familiar to me. Besides, they are supposed to be versatile, these angels, and they can bring in the specialists if they need to! For me, it's all a matter of faith and trust that they will provide the help we need when we need it most.

Immediately, we felt Michael's powerful presence and the whole room was filled with love and light. We sent love to Ted again and assured him that he was forgiven, told him it was time to let go and that he should welcome the transition with peace and joy. Then we felt his energy fading, so we thanked Archangel Michael for his help.

I wasn't finished though because I wanted to know why it had been my parents who had brought Ted along, rather than his own loved ones. This time Dad answered and it all made sense: they knew that I would not be able to meet with Ted on this side of life again yet I also needed the closure of interacting with his energy if I was to move on from the traumatic events of recent times. The love my mother held for me meant that she wanted to be involved in this final act of love and forgiveness, too. On the other side of life, our loved ones see the bigger picture and can help us in ways we could never imagine.

How was Ted able to come to me, even though he hadn't yet passed to Spirit? I don't presume to know enough about such things to explain, but there have been numerous studies carried out about what happens immediately before death. It seems that even if the body is weak and the mind unconscious, the soul's energy is still very strong. There is plenty of anecdotal evidence of people hanging on to life for hours or even days more than predicted, as they wait for a loved one to reach their side. And healers acknowledge that as the physical chakras close down before death, the last ones to go are the brow and crown chakras where the divine connection is strongest. It's as though Ted's soul knew that there was unfinished business to clear up before transition, and he needed my blessing to release his hold on life.

Exactly twenty-four hours later, he passed to Spirit. I was informed later by email, but it didn't really matter to me that I hadn't been notified immediately, either in person or by telephone. Those precious moments of connection were all the goodbyes we needed. I was able to remember my husband with love and relive the good times and happy memories. Thanks to the precious gift of forgiveness, I could now leave the past behind and move forward in my life without bitterness or regret.

Forgiveness is the gift that keeps on giving. Not only does it help us come to terms with past traumas, it continues to enhance our lives in so many ways. We no longer waste energy on people and situations that don't serve us. When we consciously practise forgiveness, we can move forward rather than replaying others' actions and staying energetically attached to the past.

In this way, we choose to savour the present moment, because now is all that really matters. We can't change the past, and worrying about what might happen in the future simply steals our joy in the here and now. We find that we are much calmer because of this energy shift and, just as importantly, this change helps those around us, too, to appreciate the value of forgiveness and dramatically improve their lives.

A Visualisation to Cleanse Negativity

Visualisation is a powerful spiritual tool in shifting our energy to a more positive perspective and improving our state of mind, especially when we're struggling with some issue.

Most of the ones offered in this book can be done in just a few minutes, but it's important to set aside time when we won't be disturbed so we can concentrate fully on what we're doing and take as long as we need. Many people find it easiest to do them first thing in the morning or last thing at night before bed, when the house is quiet and there's no risk of being disturbed by the telephone or visitors. Some find it easier to visualise than others but, like most new skills, we get better with practice; so we just need to carry on regardless because it's the shift of energy that's important, and this will still happen because that's where our focus is.

Whilst meditation and visualisation are often spoken of inter-changeably, they are totally different. Meditation is all about relaxation and inducing a state of calm by going deep into our consciousness. Here, surprising things may happen if we are receptive, or we may not even remember our meditation if we go really deep. With visualisation, on the other hand, the mind is relaxed yet always active throughout. We actively create the appropriate scenario for whatever we want to achieve, and for this we need to be alert, directing the visualisation and our energy. Also, it's easier to 'come back to the moment' than after meditation, although it's important, as with any energy work, to have a drink of water handy to ensure we are hydrated and grounded.

We begin in a relaxed state by making ourselves comfortable, either sitting or lying down, closing the eyes and doing a few cycles of breathing to release tension. Breathe in slowly through the nose for a count of three, visualising pure white healing air, then hold for a count of three before exhaling through the mouth, breathing out any tensions or stresses. Imagine the exhale as a dark colour, such as grey or dark red, and see the breath getting lighter with each exhalation as we release what no longer serves us.

***

Some difficult issues have been described in the first two chapters, so let's begin with the Fire Visualisation, to clear away and cleanse our minds of negativity. We all get weighed down sometimes by negative thoughts and it can be hard to break that cycle. Now, fire may usually be thought of as a destructive force, yet it also clears the way for new things, for new growth.

This visualisation is spectacular and very effective in shifting our thinking to the positive. (If you believe in the guidance of dragons, you may like to invite a fire dragon to help with burning up any negative thoughts.)

✳ Prepare as described above and relax with eyes closed. Either invite a fire dragon to be present, helping to burn away negative and fear-based thoughts, or imagine a bonfire kindling and growing in front of you. Some people begin to feel heat at this point, but in any case just know that the process has begun.

✳ Now see a road opening up ahead. It's black, like a regular tarmac road, and it represents our negative, fear-based thought patterns. The road travels downhill, into the lower energies.

✳ Deliberately direct the fire, or ask your dragon, to burn away these lower energies, and see the flames gradually destroy the black road that represents negative thinking. It melts and then burns as the flames chase down and destroy every inch.

✳ Take a few moments to appreciate the new feeling of lightness you have, no longer weighed down by negative, fear-based thinking.

❋ Now look to the sky and see a pink stream, like the vapour contrail of an aircraft, high above. This is 'the road of positive thought' that represents our new thinking, where everything and anything is possible. Invite this stream to descend and travel right through your head and body, clearing away any remaining negativity as it goes.

❋ Affirm that, from now on, your thinking will follow the higher road of positive thought, rather than descending the dark path of negativity.

❋ Come back into the room and have a drink of water.

CHAPTER THREE

Love Is All

What does love mean? There are so many kinds of love, and so many books and songs written and films produced with love as their central theme over the years, you'd think we would all be experts on it by now, wouldn't you? After all, there's no shortage of source material out there! Yet when it comes down to it, love means different things to each of us. We feel it on various levels and we react to it according to previous experiences, our personal perspectives and upbringing. This short word that's bandied about so freely is at the root of all sorts of confusion and has been since the first people walked the Earth.

"Love is patient, love is kind. It does not envy, it does not boast, it is not proud. It does not dishonour others, it is not self-seeking, it is not easily angered, it keeps no record of wrongs. Love does not delight in evil but rejoices with the truth. It always protects, always trusts, always hopes, always perseveres." (I Corinthians 13, verses 4 -7)

Reading this again for the first time in many years, it strikes me how relevant this passage is to the Soul Cave. This description of love is what living a spiritual life is all about, approaching everything we do from the perspective of love. That's because trying to understand love and feeling it on different levels is important to attaining the state of mind where communication with Spirit can take place. It's at the heart of all spiritual practices.

Several of my spiritual mentors and teachers believe that, in spiritual work, only two energies really matter – fear and love. Fear is a negative energy, prompted by a sense of lack or loss and by feelings such as envy, greed, jealousy, anger and bearing grudges towards others because of past hurts. Love is just the opposite, it means respecting oneself and others and celebrating their achievements, appreciating what we have rather than lamenting what we feel is missing from our life. It is about forgiving past hurts so we can let go of them and move forward. It is being unapologetic about who we are, and never giving up on oneself.

We are much happier when we can shift our energy to this perspective. When something goes wrong, for example, we can try not to cry, "Why has this happened to me?" but instead ask ourselves, "What can I learn from this?" This simple but effective shift means that we don't regard ourselves as victims of circumstance, and we are then able to persevere and look for solutions and new paths to take us forward. On the other hand, while we are in the fear perspective of "Why me?" we are focusing on the negative, and we are likely to attract more of the same into our lives.

It's a matter of cultivating an attitude of acceptance and we only achieve that through working on ourselves to maintain positive energy. In turn, that relies on loving ourselves just as we are. The element of self-love and self-acceptance is a really important aspect of spirituality.

Consider this. How many times, when something has gone wrong, do we blame ourselves for it? The thing is, if we don't respect ourselves then we can't expect other people to respect us, can we? Furthermore, we always attract what we send out, so if our energy is focused on our own perceived failings then we are sending out negativity and attracting negative people and situations into our lives. We tend to forget we are only human, and sometimes we set the bar much higher for our own achievements than we would dream of doing for others. When we inevitably fail to meet our own unrealistic expectations, we beat ourselves up about it.

That's bad enough, but now we've shifted into the energy of fear because we don't think we're good enough, and that negative energy is going to draw in more of the same. Alternatively, if we can accept that we've done our best and dispense with the self-blame, we will project an air of confidence that draws more like-minded people into our circle. It's a small shift yet it can have a big impact on the way we see ourselves and the way others perceive us.

So next time you are blaming yourself for a perceived failing, ask yourself honestly whether you did everything possible to ensure success, given the information available to you and the prevailing circumstances. If the answer is "Yes" then you have nothing to reproach yourself for. If it's a "No" then ask yourself what you could have done differently. In this way we learn necessary lessons and can store the information for future reference.

When we accept that we've made a mistake, we just need to tell ourselves that "anybody who never makes a mistake never does anything" (Theodore Roosevelt), then we can move on. It's much more helpful to analyse things in this way rather than merely judging ourselves, and once we've done it a few times it will become second nature. This is true for many aspects of energy work.

A big part of working with energy is learning to feel and acknowledge everything around us, and that includes our own emotions. This is the practice of mindfulness. And because an awareness of love is central to a path of spirituality, we can deliberately practise its development. One way to do this is through visualisation.

The example here is one that I often use with clients, especially if they are particularly missing a loved one, whether it's someone they are parted from by distance or by death. It's short and uplifting and it really works to help us become more in tune with our own feelings.

＊ First make sure that you won't be disturbed for a while and then sit comfortably with eyes closed and feet resting on the floor. Relax and place the right hand over the heart.

* Now visualise a small pinprick of pink light, focused like a laser beam, under the palm of that hand.

* See it grow slowly and spread until it fills your whole torso. You may begin to feel warmer or sense that your hand is lifting away from your heart. Don't resist these feelings, flow with them.

* Visualise the pink light expanding out of your body and surrounding you like an aura. Relax in this warm feeling for a few moments.

* Who do you want to send love to? It could be anyone, living or in the spirit world, or it could be a group of people. It may be a family member or a friend. It may even be someone whom you wish to forgive for past hurts. See them standing in front of you, neither too close nor too far away, and spend a few moments observing them, being thankful for their presence.

* Now, gently and deliberately expand your surrounding aura of pink light so that it also includes this person. See them wrapped in the light and connected to you, and enjoy the peaceful feeling that comes with this.

* When you feel ready, begin to draw the pink light back from the other person, so that first it surrounds your own body again and then grows smaller until it's back to the original pinprick of energy you started with.

* Let the hand come to rest, then open your eyes and come back to the present moment. Allow a few minutes for the energy to settle before moving your limbs. Take a drink of cool water.

With practice, we will feel as though we have truly connected with our loved ones in this way. The visualisation can be used on special days, like birthdays or anniversaries, when we are unable to be with them in person. As suggested, it can also help if we are experiencing difficulties in any of our relationships, because consciously sending love reminds us of the inner bonds we share and can even strengthen them. Many clients have reported that, after sending love like this, they have felt a softening in their own attitudes towards whomever they were experiencing difficulties with. If this is used for forgiveness, it can be helpful to add an affirmation at the end, such as, "It's over, I forgive you, let's move on", repeated three times.

Not everyone finds visualisation easy, but with practice it will come. And some may find it strange to think of using the same visualisation for forgiveness as for sending out love. But consider, forgiveness is a gift to oneself, so we are showing self-love by forgiving someone else in order to be able to move on from a situation. It doesn't mean that we have to feel love for the person we are forgiving – that is very difficult to achieve even if we aspire to it – but we do need to have love in our hearts to practise forgiveness.

Genuinely feeling things, rather than just thinking about them, gives a much deeper connection in all sorts of ways, and this is especially true when it comes to love whether it's directed to oneself or someone else. And visualisation can help us to feel things more deeply. It's an alternative to meditation, which many find difficult. It can be used in pretty much any situation and is a great tool for manifesting what we want in our lives too.

Some people have difficulty following written meditations or visualisations, so another idea is to record them on your mobile phone and then play them back. This way we can give our full attention to the practice. Spend some time finding out what works for you, and perhaps even have a go at creating your own visualisations. Just close your eyes and think of what you want to happen in your life: it could be healing, a better relationship, or even asking forgiveness for yourself for a mistake you have made. Then visualise the scene played out for you. It can be very uplifting when we just allow our subconscious to take us where it wants to go.

Anything we do as part of a spiritual life needs to be done with love if it is to achieve the results we seek. And difficult though it may be, the love we aspire to feel should come from both the heart and the mind. It should be unconditional.

This is what most pet dogs are blessed with! Look how much joy they get from life: with no expectations, they are just happy to be shown attention, fed and played with. Everything is an adventure for them. A dog doesn't agonise over what others think of him or wonder if he's good enough. When did you last see a dog check himself in the mirror before going out? He's not interested in external appearances, he just gets on with his life, taking joy in the simple things, trusting that the day will be good, and so it is. Perhaps we'd all be happier if we could be more Dog.

So what's stopping us? If we don't fret about how we look, don't worry about whether we did something right, and don't care what others think of us, three opportunities for self-criticism immediately disappear. When we love ourselves as we are, others respect us for that and it becomes easier for them to love us in turn. This is not being selfish, rather it's simply accepting ourselves and suspending self-judgement. Once we can do that for ourselves, it's not such a big step to extend the same courtesy to those around us.

Unconditional love doesn't mean that we allow everyone to get away with murder while we smile serenely and pretend that nothing has happened. It's about releasing ourselves from the need to judge others or to try and change their behaviour, accepting that it's up to them to do that. When we release the need for control, over events or other people, life becomes so much simpler and happier, not just for ourselves but for everyone else as well. We expect less from ourselves and from others, and therefore we are less likely to be disappointed.

However, this doesn't mean that we are lowering our standards. In fact it's the opposite, because we are actually raising the bar for happiness when we set the intention not to make judgements and not to anticipate results but await developments, trusting that all will work out for the best.

For some, this may sound impossible right now, and it's certainly not an easy mindset switch. It takes time, self-awareness and clear intention to embrace unconditional love, and inevitably there will be challenges to navigate and barriers to break through. But it's worth the trouble because we find that negative emotions like resentment, jealousy and anger will naturally fade away, along with our expectations. That makes for a more peaceful life. If our insides are not churning up over a perceived slight or injustice, there is more room for serenity and peace.

I know this works because I am living this way now. Well, it's not really in my nature to be covetous, jealous, or bear grudges. However, I have been guilty of holding on to the past at times and blaming myself for things that went wrong, even if there didn't seem to be any cause. I have learned that when we begin to respect ourselves more and suspend self-judgement, we find it easier to let go of the past and to practise forgiveness for ourselves and others. As a result, we find peace within, our lives are calmer and with less recrimination. Simply, we feel so much better.

All of this doesn't mean that there won't still be bad days. Life is constantly changing, up and down, and we are only human after all. The big difference is that, with love and self-acceptance, we can learn to shift the energy and either turn a bad day into a good day or at least resolve peacefully to start afresh tomorrow. Learning to give unconditional love doesn't take away life's challenges and nor should we expect that, because it's navigating these challenges that helps us to keep learning and growing. What's important is that we no longer see setbacks as disasters, and therefore we don't let them bring us down in the long term. Our change of attitude makes a big difference to how we handle difficulties when they inevitably arise.

Feeling good about ourselves impacts every area of our lives so it makes sense to work at this and ensure that feeling good is our default setting. When we understand how unconditional love works, and apply it to ourselves first and foremost, we are taking a giant step in the right direction.

Some will say that this is all too much of a challenge, especially if our lives are really stressful or self-criticism has been ingrained in us for years. That's often a result of our upbringing, so how can it be changed?

Well, it's not so difficult to make a start. One of my mentors teaches that a simple way to start feeling better about ourselves is to look in the mirror several times a day and say, "I love you", until we believe it. I gave this a go and of course felt like an idiot and kept getting the giggles at first; yet I know that it has worked for many people. An alternative is the two-pronged strategy of giving yourself a virtual pat on the back when things work out well, and telling yourself how fortunate you are to have certain things in your life. When you cook a nice meal, tell yourself that you have done well and express gratitude for being able to buy good food. When you go on an enjoyable trip, even a short one, congratulate yourself for thinking of it and remind yourself how fortunate you are to be able to go to beautiful places.

In no time at all, this way of thinking becomes natural and, when we find reasons for gratitude in everything, we start to feel good most of the time. Effectively, we are showing love for the good things in our lives and that love comes back to us in feelings of wellbeing. There are so many ways to feel better about ourselves, and along the journey to self-love and self-respect we find the old negative mindset turned around.

"Ah, but…" some will say, "we have responsibilities for others." Yes, many of us have been programmed to put other people's needs before our own and consequently we come to believe that it's selfish to give so much attention to ourselves. We need to unlearn that perspective if we are going to succeed with our inner work and live lives of happiness and joy. Self-love leads to both self-awareness and an increased awareness of the world around us. As we learn to focus on ourselves better, that clarity extends around us and we begin to see life very differently. We find ourselves more in tune with the universe and less alone with our problems, because now we see them as hurdles along our path, as opportunities for learning, rather than barriers to our happiness.

This works because the core of self-love is accepting ourselves and everything around us as it is, and working with what's there rather than trying to change or control everything. It's about playing the hand we are dealt rather than throwing it in. Once we decide not to apportion blame or acknowledge guilt, we have a clearer picture of what needs to happen for things to change. We realise that there are certain changes that we can make for ourselves whereas, when we are making judgements or feeling guilty, that cannot happen because we are dependent on the input of others.

Sometimes, then, we just have to walk away from certain situations or relationships when we realise that change is needed but nobody else seems willing or able to make it and we have no influence over their actions. My example, of course, was walking away from my husband and my marriage, despite our love, because after Paddy's death it was the only thing to do to ensure my safety and peace of mind. I couldn't influence Ted's illness.

A more common example is the need to walk away from a friendship, however longstanding, because we realise that the other person doesn't respect us. This can be difficult to do but it's important to love ourselves enough to know that we deserve better. Staying unhappy and trying to 'put things right', believing we must have done something wrong and need to make amends, simply doesn't work.

Maybe you are thinking that something doesn't quite sit right here, advocating unconditional love one minute then talking about walking away from husbands and old friends the next? If someone wants us to change and makes us feel guilty, yet we know we haven't done anything wrong, they are placing conditions on our relationship and trying to control the status quo. It's a different matter, of course, if we acknowledge our part in the situation and apologise; but if we are being made to feel that we have done something wrong when we have no idea what that is, then this is unfair judgement and expectation on the other's part. That can only come from their own feelings of fear or lack, the opposite of love, and if they cannot change their behaviour then we need to be the agent of change. For the sake of self-love and self-respect, sometimes the only thing left to do is to walk away.

Sadly, I once had to walk away from a fifty-year friendship because my friend was convinced that her husband and I were having an affair. He was also a good friend, and had simply been talking to me about problems they were having, because he was getting nowhere trying to discuss these things with his wife. He wanted to be heard. And in any case, we lived in different countries and were just talking by phone. Eventually, her hostility meant that there was no trust left between us and the situation could not be resolved. The friendship had become toxic.

Naturally, everybody's situation is unique, and whether there is any chance of retrieving harmony must be a personal choice; nobody should ever do anything that doesn't feel right for them. However, it's vital that all of us devote more time to getting to know ourselves and what we want and need from our lives, analyse what gives us joy and brings serenity, and make sure that's what we are working towards.

I believe that the only way to achieve that is through unconditional love, first for ourselves, for our own lives, and then for the world around us. When we let go of the energy of fear and begin to live in love, life is so much better. Instead of anticipating problems, we can look to the future with hope.

When it comes down to it, love is all. It is all that really matters because it's what motivates us to be kind to ourselves and to others. People who are unkind in their behaviour, their words or actions, invariably have lacked love in their lives. But, thankfully, it's never too late to learn to love.

Some readers may be wondering why so much has been devoted to 'spirituality' in these opening pages, to the philosophy of love and gratitude. After all, I am a psychic so shouldn't I be writing about the psychic gifts of, say, clairvoyance or healing? That's coming next!

It's true, of course, that developing those abilities, those gifts of the mind, does not necessarily depend on following any particular philosophy or religion. Almost everyone is capable, to some degree. And there have been many well-known mediums and healers who don't seem to have a spiritual bone in their bodies. Unpleasant characters, even, with big egos.

Personally, I don't see the value in following that sort of path because at the end of the day there's an essential ingredient missing. Without a loving and spiritual mindset, we cannot truly offer healing or guidance to others where it is really needed, at the soul level. Moreover, the good news is that when we follow a truly spiritual path, those psychic gifts often arise quite naturally!

CHAPTER FOUR

An Accidental Psychic

Many people who come to spirituality have a traumatic back story to share; dealing with major challenges often leads us to exploring our spiritual side more and connecting with who we really are. I had despaired of ever feeling normal again, and nothing I was doing to keep life on an even keel was working. But I wasn't ready to give up. There had to be an antidote to all the negativity that surrounded me and I began to find it, almost by accident, when I started to work on my psychic development. Reconciliation with the past can come when we step into the unknown and involve ourselves in unplanned events.

My own introduction to the magic and mystery of the spiritual realm was occasionally a bit scary – awakening some things within that had been left sleeping – but it was never boring. I had always been pretty open-minded, ready to acknowledge any and all viewpoints and certainly never drawn to any particular belief system. Indeed, I didn't even have much faith in myself. I soon learned, though, that there has to be an attitude of trust if we are to benefit from psychic development, because an open mind and an open heart are essential to the process. And, hand on heart, deciding to develop my psychic connections opened up a wonderful new world for me.

If you are wondering whether to do the same, I strongly advise to find a teacher or mentor that you are drawn to and go along with trust, prepared for new experiences and some (probably pleasant) surprises! After all, we are talking about natural abilities here since we all have a certain level of psychic awareness from birth. This is believed to be one of the reasons that babies smile at nothing very much, and why so many young children talk about their 'invisible friends'. Unfortunately, as we get older this instinctive ability is dampened down either by our own fear and reluctance or by other people's dismissal and ridicule. So the first step to take in psychic development, whatever one's age, is to set the intention to be open to significant 'signs' and to communication from Spirit. It can help to write this intention down and then look at it regularly to reinforce our commitment.

So what exactly is a psychic, accidental or otherwise, and is it the same as a medium? There's no tidy definition here, because working with the soul and with Spirit, which is what all psychics and mediums do to varying degrees, is not easily explained. In any case, much depends on personal experience as there are many different ways to connect with Spirit and receive messages and guidance, for oneself or for others.

The certificate I received at the end of my two-year psychic development course assures me that I can call myself a psychic and clairvoyant, yet my experience may be different to that of several others working in this field. In practice, for me, it is about reading the energy of others to learn more about their situation and, in particular, the areas of their lives where they need healing. I don't even need to be with them physically, and insights often come when messaging friends or even strangers on social media.

For example, I was once chatting with a gentleman who was enquiring about an online oracle card reading. He told me that he'd ended a long-term relationship some time ago and now felt sad that he was "destined to be single". I didn't know anything else about him, only his name and the town he lived in. However, I had a clear sense of familiarity and newness, that he would be getting together with someone he already knew and very soon; he would attend a regular activity with this person, rather than joining a group of friends as usual, and the relationship would develop into something more.

Shortly afterwards, he messaged me to say that he'd bumped into a neighbour on the stairs of their apartment block on his way to the local quiz night. They knew each other though only slightly. She asked where he was going and whether she could tag along, as the friend she was supposed to meet had cancelled their evening out at short notice. The couple subsequently dated and my client now felt far more positive about his future, realising that he shouldn't just assume there was "nobody out there" for him.

What had happened here? I had picked up from his energy that he needed a boost to his self-esteem, and had seen possibilities for him when he saw only loneliness ahead. Here we have a blend of psychic awareness (energy) and clairvoyance (seeing), with an element of emotional healing too.

At other times, I am able to tune into the spirit energy around people and pass on a comforting or constructive message from a loved one who has passed over. This is mediumship at work. In all cases, it's about working with energy and helping people with the healing they need. Even though a spirit message may appear superficial, the contact can have a big impact on the recipient.

An acquaintance of mine, Veronica, discovered that her son had died in bed from a heart attack. He was only in his mid-twenties and had seemed to be quite healthy. Some months later, I had a stall selling crystals at a local market and I saw Veronica walking towards me. In broad daylight, I could also see the shadow of a young man behind her with his arm draped across her shoulders, and I realised that this was her late son, although we'd never met. I heard the name 'Gerry' in my head. Realising that I could see him, he told me that his mother had looked at several pairs of shoes and was going to go back and buy the red ones; she never could decide right away.

As she approached, I hugged her and told her that Gerry was with her, his arm around her shoulders, and I passed on his message. She gasped, saying that Gerry had always joked about her not being able to make her mind up, especially when it came to shoes. And, whenever they had been together, he would drape his arm around her shoulders exactly as I'd seen.

Veronica told me that she hadn't been able to stop thinking that her son must have been scared, in pain and alone at the time of his passing. I started to explain my belief that no soul leaves this world alone and scared, that the transition is peaceful, when Gerry interrupted to say that he'd just slipped away in his sleep so he didn't want her to worry on that score. This was just a small mother-and-son moment – and the spirit message wasn't exactly deeply philosophical – but it meant the world to Veronica and it helped her greatly in processing her grief.

Have you ever felt the presence of a loved one soon after their passing? And did you enjoy the moment or dismiss it as wishful thinking? It can be very soothing and healing just to be still in that moment, and tell them how much they are loved and missed. This is especially so if their passing was sudden and you had no opportunity to say goodbye. Experienced mediums say that whenever we think of a loved one in spirit, we bring them closer, and that's a lovely thought to hold onto.

Sometimes we can receive great comfort in the most unexpected circumstances. Several years ago, a friend passed away suddenly in Spain. Stevie was universally liked for his kind, helpful nature and his extensive charity work. In that country, funerals take place within a few days and the paperwork is sorted out later. (This practice dates back to the time before refrigeration when it was practical to bury the dead as soon as possible because of the heat. The police are called first to unexpected deaths, to rule out foul play, and then a doctor certifies death and the family can proceed with the funeral without delay.) Stevie passed on Friday and the funeral was the next afternoon.

I went along with a mutual friend and, unusually, the coffin was open. The first and last person I had ever seen in a coffin was my father, decades earlier when I was a teenager, and the trauma of his subsequent cremation had skewed my views about funerals. I was always adamant that I didn't want to be cremated myself. It was certainly not my intention to view Stevie in his coffin yet, as people filed past, I felt compelled to join them. Then, as I regarded my friend, I simultaneously felt his presence behind me. He was palpably excited at how many people had turned up!

"I can't believe all these people showed up for me," he exclaimed. "I don't even know half of them, and I thought I knew everybody around here."

There was standing room only in the huge chapel. I told Stevie that he'd touched so many lives, it was no wonder people had turned up in force to say goodbye. He asked me to tell his best friend, who had just delivered a moving eulogy, that he was okay now. Then he had another important message… for me.

"You know that's not me in there, right?"

I nodded. Of course, it is at the heart of my beliefs that the body is just a container for the soul, and Stevie was proving it here only twenty-four hours after his own transition.

"So what's all this about saying in your Will you don't wanna be cremated, girl? Don't matter what they do with me now. I still know what's going on with my friends and family, don't I? Let it go and save yourself some cash."

I was astounded by this message. Only my close family knew about that clause in my Will, but Stevie had picked up on it and realised this throwback to my father's death was something I needed to release. But was I maybe having this conversation with myself, not with Stevie, seeing him there having brought back dark memories from years ago?

Just then the friend accompanying me, who is also spiritually aware, said that he could also sense Stevie's energy around him and joked that he seemed to be having a final walkabout. It was all the confirmation I needed and I finally understood that, despite every-thing I'd learned on my spiritual journey, I had yet to heal from the situation around my father's death. This time, the message from Spirit was helping me to begin that process.

Sometimes, spirit connections can simply be great fun, you're not being 'of service' and there's no obvious 'message' to be delivered; it can just be an experience to enjoy and further confirmation of the continuity of life. This happened when my family and I visited St Mawes Castle near Truro in Cornwall. We were in the garrison Mess, where the soldiers used to relax, and although it was a hot April day there was a decided chill in the air. The rest of the family decided they were going outside to warm up again but I thought I knew what was behind the change in temperature and, sure enough, I sensed a presence close by.

"Hello, nice to meet you, I'm Sandra," I said.

"Well met, my lady," a male voice answered. "Thou art comely indeed." I was being flirted with by a soldier from history! He was speaking in Old English, from the Tudor period. "I am called for the king. My name is Henry."

There hasn't been another King Henry since Henry VIII passed in 1547, and St Mawes Castle was built in the 1540s. Being 'called for' someone was an expression meaning, as we would say, being 'named after'. Henry then accompanied me on the rest of our tour of the castle, telling me that he loved to see people enjoying the place where he'd been so happy, although it wasn't very often that he was able to communicate with his visitors. He also told me a few things that weren't in the guidebook, so I was able to impress my family with my depth of knowledge. (I didn't confide the source. They're more or less comfortable with me talking to dead people, but prefer me to do it when they're not nearby!)

Anyone who is open to spiritual development can also experience psychic connections like these, perhaps sensing spirits in the house or seeing loved ones in dreams, even if it was many years ago when we had imaginary friends in childhood. We never lose that connection and it's there to be developed whenever we are ready.

At a spirit art demonstration in Plymouth, I discovered the identity of my own long-ago imaginary friends. At this event, a spirit artist was guided to draw portraits of loved ones in the afterlife, while a medium tuned into the spirit energy and brought through messages for those audience members who recognised the drawings. One portrait reminded me of someone, but I wasn't sure who it was. Then the medium laughed out loud as he asked the lady how she had passed over.

"I ran out of breath," she said.

I knew then that the portrait was my maternal grandmother, showing herself as a young woman. Nobody else recognised the drawing or the quirky message, but I had heard it many times as a child. Whenever my parents attended a funeral, my brother and I would stay with Gran; and whenever I asked the inevitable question about how the person had died, her response was always, "They ran out of breath."

Gran went on to confirm the identity of my own childhood 'invisible friends', two little girls called Gwendoline and Marjory. They were my mother's twin sisters who had passed over at the age of six months from scarlet fever. It was so lovely for me to finally identify them properly.

My Gran then wasted no time in telling the medium that it was about time I finally got going on my spiritual path, as she'd known when I was five years-old that this was my destiny. Her surprising revelations served as welcome confirmation that I was following the right path when, in middle age, I'd finally enrolled on an accredited psychic development course.

If these accounts fire your enthusiasm to deepen your own understanding of the spiritual world, you may be wondering how to go about it safely. It's important to have 'an open mind and an open heart' but we also need to know that we can trust our teachers. There is a lot of information on the Internet, for example, but is it what you want and, more importantly, is it what you really need for your personal development? We all know that there's a lot of misinformation on the Internet too. I was lucky enough to discover two excellent mentors, one in England and one in Spain, and I believe we are drawn to our ideal teachers when the timing is right.

As we look to learn about spirituality and psychic development, it's a good idea to check for local spiritualist churches and spiritual groups in the local Press or on social media. Going along to meetings or services, perhaps sitting quietly at the back to start with, and getting to know the speakers and mediums who serve there is a good way to get a flavour of what's happening locally without being too involved until it feels safe and the right place to be. We can also head to the local New Age shop or bookstore. The owners of these are usually very knowledgeable and can put us in touch with accredited people who run courses, groups or development circles.

However, before joining any course or circle it's a good idea to join a meditation class, as this plays a big part in regular spiritual practice. Apart from its proven benefits for our physical health, meditation is an excellent way to expand our natural psychic talents since it helps to clear the mind in order to recognise signs, messages and information from Spirit. It's also very helpful in daily life, training us to keep calm, to stay clear of drama and anger, and to set our thoughts in order whatever may be happening around us.

There are many forms of meditation, from guided journeys to simple breathing techniques, and a good teacher will be willing to explain everything until we find out what works best for us. Starting out, I was advised that meditation would help me accept what was happening in life and respond to events in a calmer way. The development of psychic abilities then followed on from the insights and inner peace I gained from meditation, an unexpected but very welcome bonus.

I am fortunate to be able to go very deeply into meditation now and literally take myself into another world while the universe works on my soul. This has actually caused hilarity in some circles I've attended, always being the last one to 'return to the room' and sometimes ending up folded over double in my chair, touching my toes. When the group leader told me this, I didn't believe her because I'm just not that flexible, but she had the photographic evidence to prove it.

One time, we'd all just slipped into our meditation when the doorbell rang, much to everyone else's annoyance. It was a man from the local Council who had been sent to test the smoke alarms, which he did several times while chatting to the other ladies in the circle. Normal service was eventually resumed and the meditation continued. Afterwards, the group leader apologised for the interruption but I was completely mystified. What interruption? Somehow, I'd managed to stay in the meditation throughout it all.

Of course, this sort of thing doesn't happen for everyone and some find it difficult at first to settle into meditation, but we soon discover what works best for us. There are many free guided meditations on YouTube, for example, and we should follow whatever we are drawn to. Most psychic development circles also include meditation in each session. As we get used to the process, we become calmer and the benefits continue into every part of our lives.

Psychic development circles help us to identify and develop our natural psychic skills whilst at the same time teaching the basics of the main 'clair' senses (clairvoyance, and so on). We enhance our intuition and learn how to work with the chakras, how to read oracle cards and how to use everyday items such as flowers, sand, ribbons or drawings to encourage spiritual awareness. All this is achieved with various exercises and fun games along with some study and note-taking, but mostly it's interactive and enjoyable for everyone. Circle is usually a closed group, with the same people attending each time.

Most psychic practice depends on using one or other of the clairs, sometimes several of them working together to bring through inform-ation. At circle, there will be exercises to identify each person's strongest ability and that will be worked with first to build confidence, others developing later as appropriate.

* **Clairvoyance** means 'clear seeing', enabling us to see visions in our minds of the past, present or future. The information picked up is often very detailed. For example, the Tarot reader who saw my dog Luna was able to describe her very accurately, as well as her location.

❋ **Clairaudience**. We may hear songs, music or words, perhaps in the form of messages. I have often heard songs before reading for people, then discovered that it was the favourite song of a deceased loved one. The sounds may be inside the head or even, for some people, seem to be within the room.

❋ **Clairsentience**. This is a clear feeling not unlike 'gut instinct' or strong intuition, so it is often the easiest skill to work with at first as we all have some familiarity with it. It's certainly very helpful in accessing important information about a person or situation. A lady came to my stall to buy some crystals and I immediately sensed that she was being treated unfairly at work. She didn't understand this at the time, but later messaged me to say she'd been offered a job that she'd previously been turned down for; the employer admitted he'd been wrong to reject her.

❋ **Claircognisance**. Sometimes we just know something without any rational explanation, maybe a premonition, a warning, or something important in a client's character or demeanour during a reading. This takes a lot of faith to work with, because we usually don't know why or how we know the information, even though it could be important.

❋ **Clairalience** and **Clairgustance** are the rarer abilities to smell or taste something that doesn't have a physical origin, such as when I smell my father's favourite cigarettes in a non-smoking environment or the favourite drink of a client's deceased loved one. A friend of mine regularly smells her late husband's after-shave when there's no-one around, and finds it very comforting.

Another important part of psychic development is learning divination, through 'reading' cards or something else like drawings, ribbons, flowers or sand; I have even seen flour and sugar used for readings! Traditionally, of course, there have been many psychics who used tealeaves (tasseomancy) or crystal balls (crystallomancy or, more simply, scrying) for divination. All of these items are tools that help us, by psychic intuition, to gain insights into someone's character, their immediate concerns and perhaps their hopes and fears for the future.

One common exercise used at development circles is to ask everyone to draw an image, something simple like a tree or a house, and then other members of the circle will see what they can divine from the drawing – its size and style, the colours used and other clues. When the exercise is repeated after a few months, the changes are usually surprising: the inner work done will mean that drawings change and people are able to give more confident and detailed insights. This exercise can also be done with writing, clearing the mind and then writing down whatever comes. These things all help with learning how our minds work and the issues we may need to work through to clear energy blocks.

Becoming familiar with Tarot, angel and oracle cards, and understanding the differences between them, is an important skill. A circle or course leader should cover the practicalities of how to choose the deck or decks that suit each person, how to cleanse and bless the cards, and how to prepare oneself for readings as well, of course, as the interpretation of cards. There is, then, no substitute for practice. Usually the members of a group will do short readings for one another, and with more work at home with family and friends one soon becomes familiar and confident with the mechanics of conducting a reading.

What about taking an online course? There are some excellent ones available but naturally there aren't the interactive and social elements of attending a development group in person. If this is your chosen route, though, perhaps because you are shy about working with strangers or there isn't a suitable group in your area, do look for courses with video training and live seminars so that you can see things in action, ask questions and link to other students. These courses can be expensive, so it's important to read reviews, check out the prospectus, and make sure it at least covers the basics described here.

It's a bit of a leap from having a vague interest in psychic matters to actually getting fully involved in a development course; even then, not everyone will want to take things further or work professionally.

That's perfectly fine, because spirituality is deeply personal and we are drawn to it for different reasons. The main one, I believe, is because we need to heal, whether that be psychologically, emotionally or spiritually. And we can't do it alone. On a course or in circle, we may learn about many aspects of psychic work yet not everything will be appealing or come naturally. So it's fine to choose wherever we want our journey to take us, guided by our instincts and signs received from Spirit.

For example, as described here, I've worked as both psychic and medium and many interactions with clients involve elements of both. However, I now prefer to concentrate on reading cards and working with a client's energy, rather than doing demonstrations of mediumship or serving as a bridge between the two worlds. I feel that I can be of service to more people this way. At a demonstration of mediumship, everyone is looking for a message and many will go away disappointed, because the medium can only do so much in the allotted time and in any case no medium can guarantee to bring through a particular soul, or even anyone!

Once we decide to develop our psychic abilities, we come to understand that we can control our own energy, we can begin to find our power and live the life we deserve.

A Visualisation for Grounding

Grounding is a practice to balance the physical and spiritual energies in the body and connect with the Earth so that we feel more focused and present in the moment. It is important for everyone but it particularly matters when we make the choice to work with our psychic abilities. Being grounded means our thoughts aren't flying off every which way, and we're not adversely affected by others' energy or what's happening around us. It also stops us from overthinking; we become more aligned with our feelings, our intuition is boosted and we feel a lot more at ease, more of the time.

Some people like to make sure they are grounded every day, as soon as they wake and before doing anything else. It becomes part of the morning routine, like taking a shower and brushing teeth, and helps us to be in the best frame of mind to start the day.

✳ Sit in a comfortable chair, with feet on the floor and back straight. It's important for the feet to be in contact with the ground, and even better if the exercise can be done outside with bare feet on the grass or the earth or a wooden deck.

✳ Visualise the soles of the feet producing roots, extending deeper and deeper into Mother Earth. Some may feel a pulling sensation as the roots extend down – this is good, don't fight it. Send those roots further and further down until they reach a huge crystal in the centre of the Earth. This crystal can be any kind you like, but clear quartz is best as it is the master healer. (There's more on the properties of various crystals later in this book.)

✳ See these roots entwine around the crystal, anchoring you to the Earth and emphasising your natural connection to the universe and everything in it. Send any stress or negativity you may be holding onto down along the roots into the Earth so it can be cleansed and transmuted. You could visualise it as grey water, flushing out your body.

✳ Now the crystal sends pure white healing light up through the roots and into your body. Feel that lightness entering through the soles of your feet and filling you to the top of the head and down the arms to the tips of the fingers.

✳ Take a few moments to relax and enjoy the feeling, then slowly retract the roots from around the crystal and visualise them travelling up through the Earth and back to the feet. At this point, you may even feel the soles of the feet relax their grip.

✳ Take a few deep breaths and open your eyes. Have a drink of water. You are now fully grounded and ready to start your day!

CHAPTER FIVE

An Accidental Healer

Do you believe that ordinary people can help others to heal physically and emotionally, with no medical or other training? This was a mystery to me for many years, but then 'things happened' to me and others around me, things that just can't be explained rationally, that changed my perspective. I have had no training in healing (which is why I'm an accidental healer) yet I have been privileged to be able to help others on their healing journeys. However, I know very well that I am not the source of the healing, I am only a channel for healing energy that comes, I believe, from the universe, or Source.

Whilst a doctor uses medical knowledge to diagnose and treat illness, healers work with energy and intuition (and perhaps help from the spirit world) to bring healing where it's needed most. Healers should not normally attempt diagnosis; perhaps the most famous spiritual healer, Harry Edwards, would say that his healing guides in Spirit diagnosed the problem because they could see the bigger picture. He would then just move his hands where they were directed and pass on his guides' instructions for after-care.

Thus spiritual healing does not aim to treat specific symptoms or body parts. It's an holistic, whole-body approach to improving general wellbeing and relieving stress so that the body can relax and allow its natural healing responses such as the immune system to do what they are designed for and fight threats to the body's health like infections and hormone imbalances.

> To repeat, a spiritual healer does not heal! He or she is a channel for energy that helps a client to heal themselves.

There are many, many stories of healers who have apparently worked miracles, the most famous historically being Jesus (there are at least forty episodes of healing recorded in the Bible) whilst in modern times healers such as Harry Edwards, Edgar Cayce and Matthew Manning have helped to bring spiritual healing to the world's attention. Their undoubted successes have resulted in acceptance of healing as a valid complementary therapy in the range of treatments available in health services.

Harry Edwards (1893 – 1976) was an English spiritual healer who practised in an accessible way, by the laying-on of hands, for ordinary people whether they had spiritual beliefs or none.

"My healing is not faith healing," he said. "It's a divine gift from God to all His children and there is no disease that can't be helped in some way by spiritual healing."

In 1964 a film was made of Edwards and other healers that looked at the treatment of several people, following up a few weeks later to determine whether the healing effects were lasting. For example, two year-old Billy couldn't raise his arms due to an unidentified condition existing from birth. He was in constant pain and distress, yet after a few minutes of treatment by Edwards was able to move his arms to some degree. In the follow-up interview, he was much happier and now freely moving his previously paralysed arms whilst also more alert than he had ever been, according to his mother.

David had contracted polio at the age of three and was unable to walk without the aid of a caliper and crutches. He discarded his caliper immediately after treatment, using only the crutches, and six weeks later he was able to take his dog for increasingly long walks as the wasted muscles of his legs were strengthening.

American mystic Edgar Cayce (1877 – 1945) is often called the father of modern holistic medicine. His working method, earning him the nickname The Sleeping Prophet because of his thousands of predictions about world affairs, was to lie on a couch and go into a trance-like state in which he seemed to gain insights into the minds and bodies of his patients. He did have a close friend who was a doctor, yet his correct diagnoses and prescriptions often surprised the medical profession.

In trance, he often advocated the use of blood tests in diagnosis and spoke about the importance of drinking lots of water and following what we now recognise as the Mediterranean diet. In many ways he was ahead of his time in his health-related pronouncements.

There are numerous forms of healing now, some requiring a blend of training and intuition like Reiki, in which hand placements are important to the therapy. This is actually an ancient practice, Tibetan Buddhist in origin, rediscovered and developed by Japanese academic Dr Mikao Usui (1865 – 1926) in the early twentieth century. The name means 'universal life energy', thought of as an intelligent and loving force that knows what the causes of disharmony are in living beings and how to heal them. It is especially effective for pain relief, to ease tensions and restore balance of the body's energy, and has been proven to work at a distance. Again, Reiki energy is drawn through, not from, the healer.

All genuine Reiki Masters should be able to trace their lineage back to Mikao Usui since the system of initiation is like a family tree. It's an excellent way to confirm that a practitioner's skills are verified. The attunement of Reiki healers focuses on the importance of living in the present moment and following the Five Principles: "Just for today, I will not be angry... I will not worry... I will be grateful... I will work honestly... I will be kind to every living being..." Each day is recognised as a new opportunity for spiritual growth.

These principles are fine guidelines for all of us on a spiritual path and can help us with self-healing. Managing our own energy to avoid anger and worry, being grateful for what we have, finding joy in what we do and practising kindness all help us to achieve inner peace, whatever is happening in everyday life around us.

For Matthew Manning (b.1955), who has been practising spiritual healing since the 1970s, labels are not important. In a television interview in 2010, he said, "Healing is… about intention. The source of all healing is the same – it comes from Upstairs." He has never received any training yet is credited with amazing results over the years, always inviting and encouraging medical observation and willingly submitting himself to various tests, all of which have reflected favourably on him.

His client testimonials are impressive and in many cases he has achieved results where doctors had failed, including a client who had displaced vertebrae and was in constant pain with restricted movement for years. After just one session with Matthew, she noticed a big improvement and a year later, when she returned with an unconnected issue, there had been no recurrence of her spinal issue.

One of the most impressive examples of Matthew's healing involved a lady called Marguerite who had secondary breast cancer and had been given less than a year to live. When she came for treatment, she brought along her dachshund, Barney; he had an impacted slipped disk and the vet had recommended euthanasia since the dog could hardly move. But Marguerite never asked for healing for Barney, she just wanted him with her all the time as comfort for them both. Manning didn't touch the dog, who remained in Marguerite's lap.

The next morning, Marguerite and her husband were awoken by strange noises and found Barney running around the kitchen, tail wagging as though nothing was wrong. His X-rays were normal and the vet could offer no explanation for his sudden recovery. Moreover, Marguerite lived for more than twenty-five years following her terminal diagnosis.

These examples make a strong case for the efficacy of spiritual healing, especially as dogs and toddlers have no religious faith and Cayce wasn't even conscious during his work. Something that all these and other healers have in common is that they work with energy, the patient's, the healer's, and what is often referred to as 'universal energy', as yet not understood by science.

What happens in a healing session? Individual experiences will be different but the most important thing is that one should be relaxed and comfortable throughout, fully clothed and usually on a treatment bed or sitting on a comfortable chair. Most healers work with light hand movements on various parts of the body, with no pain or pressure, and sometimes without any direct touch. Their job is to hold a safe space for healing energy to flow.

Some people experience heat or cold from the healer's hands, and tingling or a light pulse in various parts of the body. Most relax into a meditative state, although still aware of what's happening around them, and feel more relaxed and less stressed for several days following the session.

When we are under stress of any kind, our bodies automatically trigger the Sympathetic Nervous System (SNS), getting us ready for 'fight or flight' whatever the cause. Unfortunately, the body can't tell the difference between being chased by a wild boar and hounded by a critical boss or being overdrawn at the bank, so this mechanism kicks in anyway, increasing the load on our vital organs. The SNS prevents our bodies from healing themselves, so we are spending more time stressed out than chilling out.

Spiritual healing or Reiki seem to reset the balance by activating the Parasympathetic Nervous System (PNS), so that the heartrate slows down, production of the stress hormones epinephrine and cortisol stops, and the body returns to the 'rest and digest' state in which it is able to renew and repair cells since there is no longer stress on the organs.

There are a number of regulatory bodies and professional associations for healers, with high standards of conduct and ethics for their members. But although many reputable healers do belong to such associations, there is currently no legal requirement for registration to practise as a healer. For more information, it's wise to approach one of the associations or go along with personal recommendation.

Any healer should always explain beforehand how a treatment is likely to unfold and describe the source of the energy they connect with, be that angels, spirit guides or universal energy. It's important to be happy and comfortable with one's chosen healer and their methods.

Several weeks after experiencing a stroke, my friend Gill's mental health was not good. Although she was doing well with her rehabilitation and was only slightly physically disabled, she was frustrated because changes in the brain caused by the stroke meant she had to relearn balance and coordination, and she also had difficulty remembering things. She felt like a toddler learning to walk and, with constant fatigue, she was stressed and depressed. Everything worth living for, it seemed, was being taken away. This was difficult to handle as she's a retired nurse and is more used to caring for people than receiving help herself.

Our friend Alice offered her a Reiki treatment as another option to aid recovery. During the session, Gill experienced tingling all over her body and she became more and more relaxed, to the point where it felt like she was being held close and rocked to sleep like a child. Interestingly, Alice never actually touches her clients but, on some level, Gill clearly needed the comfort of contact.

After the session, Gill felt far more optimistic about her recovery and not so alone. Whenever she felt depression coming on over the coming weeks, she remembered the sensation of being held and it helped her to a more positive frame of mind. She was more accepting of her situation, she slept better and her appetite improved.

That tingling was my own clue to discovering that I had healing hands when I visited my friend Janet in hospital after her knee replacement surgery. She was in considerable pain and I fervently wished I could help her somehow. No sooner had the thought occurred than my right hand started tingling and I had an irresistible urge to move it towards her knee.

"I don't know what's happening," I said, "I just feel I should hover my hand over your knee."

Understandably, Janet was rather alarmed at the prospect yet was in so much pain she was ready to try anything. She let me go with my instincts provided I didn't touch that knee!

I had no idea what to expect so I relaxed, closed my eyes and waited. Soon, I sensed the room filling with emerald green light, the sensation in my hand intensified and I felt Janet relaxing. After what felt like ages but was actually just a few minutes, the energy seemed to ebb away slowly and I realised we were nearing the end of the healing.

Janet opened her eyes, gingerly moved her leg, and was delighted to find there was no real pain, just a little discomfort. Within twenty-four hours she no longer needed analgesics and she made a speedy, uncomplicated recovery from the surgery. (My own belief is that we were in the presence of Archangel Raphael, the healing angel, but not everyone will share that way of thinking.)

Another significant result was with Simon, a good friend who supports my work and believes in the afterlife but definitely couldn't see how angels could fix what his doctor and physiotherapist were unable to. For some time he'd had a problem with one of his hands following a shoulder injury, and his doctor wasn't optimistic about a recovery. Simon sits at a computer for most of his working day and his painful hand was disruptive, also often disturbing his sleep.

At a barbeque with Simon, his wife Andrea and other friends, I could see he was clearly in pain. Then I felt that tingling in my hand again and saw a green glow all around him... I knew I was being guided to give healing, but there were two problems: we were in a public place and Simon didn't believe in the power of healing so was unlikely to agree. However, I reckoned without the determination of Andrea, who was "Bloody fed up of him moaning about that hand." We solved the other problem by Simon placing his hand between mine, under the table and out of sight.

As I channeled healing, I felt Simon relaxing next to me and knew we were getting somewhere. The treatment only lasted about five minutes but his hand immediately felt much better; he slept better that night and, two weeks later, he still had not felt any more pain. Three years later, there hadn't been a single episode of pain or numbness in his hand and he was now an enthusiastic convert to healing.

My friend Bev tells of an extraordinary healing back in the 1960s when she was a young student nurse, and the memory stayed with her because she met the patient again some years later in very different circumstances. Emily was only a teenager but she was dying. After several surgeries to treat severe pancreatitis, she was prone to recurring infections and her doctors said nothing more could be done. As she lay unconscious and unresponsive due to blood poisoning, her parents brought in a spiritual healer "as a last resort". They were willing to try anything to save their daughter, even though they were neither spiritual nor religious.

The healer laid his hands on Emily for only a short time, but within hours there were signs of improvement in her condition and she made a complete recovery. Everyone involved in her care, including Bev, had expected her to die and her doctors could give no medical explanation for the turnaround. It seemed that spiritual healing had brought about recovery when all reasonable hope had been lost.

Fast forward about seven years, Bev was now a district midwife and was delighted to welcome Emily as a patient, especially after the heartbreak of facing certain death a while before. Emily bore a healthy child by Caesarean Section, and heavy scarring on her abdomen was the only legacy of her traumatic teenage illness. The joy of her miraculous and enduring recovery has stayed with Bev for over half a century.

Until that day in the hospital with Janet, I'd assumed that to be a healer one had to be trained and learn special stuff, like a doctor at Medical School. I'd enjoyed Reiki sessions and other complementary therapies myself, but I never imagined that my own untrained hands could also be used for healing. Now it's my firm belief that we can all work with and manage energy and therefore we all have the capacity to heal and to be healed. My own accidental discovery of this gift is testimony to that.

We don't need any special qualifications or to come from a spiritual background, we just need to recognise the possibilities and be prepared to work on developing them. We are all part of the universe and we all tap into the same universal energy, enabling us to have healing potential. Naturally, the more we learn about it – and there are many training courses available – the more we understand about healing and energy. For some, there is also an awareness of the spirit world at work.

There are times when it is not possible for a healer to be with their client, who may be, say, in another country or an isolation ward. So it is both wonderful and extraordinary that absent healing can be just as effective as hands-on. The sanctuary that Harry Edwards created still offers absent healing by way of The Healing Minute, when at 10.00 a.m. UK time many people around the world focus their intentions on healing and world peace. Other well-known healers also have regular times to offer absent healing and it's practised in all healing circles.

As Matthew Manning says, healing is about our intention above all, so we just have to think of the person we want to send healing to and focus our caring thoughts on them. Some like to visualise healing energy streaming out to the person in need, or ask Archangel Raphael's healing rays to find them and do their work.

It's a great feeling to be able to help others by acting as a channel for healing and I never forget that I am simply an instrument, always thanking Spirit and the angels for their help. And when my clients thank me for healing, I gently remind them that I am not responsible: it's a collaboration of energies that brings about the necessary changes for healing to take place on many levels.

Let's close this chapter with a self-healing visualisation that helps us to connect with our bodies and their healing needs. It's a simple practice that we can use whenever we feel we need help to cope with physical or emotional pain.

A Healing Visualisation with Archangel Raphael

Find a comfortable and quiet place where you won't be disturbed for at least fifteen or twenty minutes, then relax with eyes closed and focus the attention in the present moment by conscious slow breathing. Visualise clear white light being breathed in for a count of three, held for three, then exhale any tension and stress for a count of three. The breath exhaled has a dark colour and it lightens each time your troubles are breathed out until it is almost clear.

✸ Visualise yourself in your 'happy place', perhaps a beach, a forest, a beautiful garden or a sunlit terrace, where you feel relaxed and connected with everything around you. You may be in a comfortable chair, reclining in a sun lounger or hammock, or lying directly on grass or sand, feeling its softness around your body and your hands and bare feet. You may be floating on a lake or in a pool, with your body weight supported.

✸ Enjoy these surroundings for a while. You may hear birds singing, the breeze through the trees or the lapping of waves. What's the weather like? Settle into the scene you have created and know that you are perfectly safe.

✸ Invite Archangel Raphael, the healing angel, to come into your special place and bring healing on all levels, physically and emotionally. You may feel his presence around you but don't worry if you don't sense him, healing will still happen. If you are aware of him, notice how he appears or how his energy feels.

✸ Visualise the crown of your head opening like a small window and observe bright white energy slowly entering, then descending through your entire body and down the arms and legs. Enjoy the feeling of warmth and light spreading through every cell of your being.

✸ Now Archangel Raphael brings in his emerald green healing ray at the crown, combining with the white energy to bring relaxation and release from stress, tension and physical and emotional pain. Pay particular attention to where this emerald ray reaches in your body, the places where you need healing, and allow a little time for it to work its magic.

✸ Feel the release of tension around your forehead and see the healing ray swirl around the eyes, bringing clarity to see things as they really are. Now it works its way around your ears, mouth and throat, helping you to speak your truth and to hear truth from others, cutting through illusion and self-deception.

* As the angelic ray moves into your shoulders and down your arms, feel it relieving any pain and inflammation in your joints, literally taking the weight of decision and anxiety from your shoulders. Your fingers may tingle now.

* The ray moves into your heart and lungs, bringing serenity and relieving stress, making breathing easier and helping the heart heal from sorrow or grief. Allow time to feel this inner peace spread throughout your entire being.

* The healing energy moves to the abdomen and through the digestive system, washing away nausea and easing physical discomfort. It continues travelling down the spine and into the hips, warming and strengthening the bones and joints, then travels into the legs, through the knees and into the feet to the tips of the toes.

* Feel the warmth and strength of the emerald green ray as your whole body is now filled with its healing energy. Visualise the crown of your head close over to keep the energy where it's needed. Relax into the sensations you feel, lighter, more relaxed and fully at ease in mind and body.

* When you are ready, give thanks for your healing and to Archangel Raphael for working with you. Spend a while enjoying your surroundings before saying farewell to your special place for now, then return to the room. Move your fingers, toes and limbs a bit, and have a drink of water.

This is a deeply relaxing meditation and you should find any aches and pains you had have now eased. We naturally tend to tense against pain, which only make it worse. You will feel less stressed, worries may not seem so serious, and your new clarity of mind will help you find solutions to the problems of everyday life.

CHAPTER SIX

Meet the Chakras

Sally always gives off an air of self-confidence yet I felt that the energy in her solar plexus area was 'stagnant' so I asked whether she was having some sort of crisis of confidence, this chakra being related to self-worth. She burst into tears! Then she told me she was having serious worries about her life's dream of building a house with her husband Colin on land they had bought. Things weren't happening as well as they hoped and they were beginning to feel a lot of negativity in the situation, wondering whether they would ever realise their dreams.

When I'd guided her through a chakra clearing visualisation, which helps people connect with their bodies and their energy, she felt more relaxed and positive about the future and the next day told me she'd had the best night's sleep in months. In a session like this, clients often say they can feel the chakras spinning and I can also feel their energy shifting. Indeed, Sally was convinced I was laying hands on her body at the chakra points, although my hand was about three inches above her body all the time.

Until I learned to meditate at the start of my Soul Cave journey, I didn't even know I had any chakras! Guided meditations often begin with the 'opening' and 'clearing' of the chakras; healers talk about chakras and 'energy flow'; a therapist may suggest that one or more of our chakras needs 'working on'. What are we talking about here, and how can we maintain why are the chakras important in our spiritual journey and how we can maintain them in the best possible condition?

The ancient Hindu belief in chakras as invisible energy centres of the human body was recorded in written form in the Vedas, among the oldest religious texts in existence, many centuries BCE. Before that, the core beliefs and instructions contained in the writings were passed down orally, so the philosophy of chakras is very ancient. There are four volumes of Vedas, each divided into four parts; one of these parts, the Upanishads, focuses on spiritual enlightenment and there we find the first information about chakras.

Later Vedic writings developed the concept of an extensive, inter-linked chakra system. The seven main chakras most therapists refer to today were described in the 16th century by Swami Purananda in his text, *Sat-Cakra-Nirupana*. This actually translates as 'description of the six centres', but six- or seven-centre systems were thought of as the same, since some believed the crown chakra not to be an energy centre as such because it was outside the body.

Traditionally, Hinduism related the chakras to mantras, elements and deities. It wasn't until 1977 that the familiar rainbow colours were assigned to the chakras by Christopher Hill in his book *Nuclear Evolution*. Hill's book also associated personality traits to each chakra, drawing on New Age ideas and philosophies. Since then, many Western therapists have begun to use appropriately coloured crystals when working with the chakras, and may use pendulums as a visible indicator of energy levels, but these add-ons are not part of the original beliefs. Nonetheless, some people are sensitive to the qualities of crystals and find they help them understand the chakras better.

Learning about this energy system is very beneficial in healing work, helping us to understand better how the mind and the body act in harmony. For practical purposes, it's usual to work with the seven main chakras, which are located in the torso from the base of the spine to the top of the head. There are a great number of chakras throughout the body, though, including several in the hands; if you hold your hands about an inch apart and move them slowly, you'll feel a tingling sensation – tangible evidence of the body's subtle energy at work. With practice, scanning the chakras by hovering the palm over their respective locations helps us become more familiar with how this energy feels.

So what exactly is a chakra? The Sanskrit word means 'wheel', believed to spin clockwise, continuously regulating the flow of energy throughout the body. The chakras interact together and although our energy is in constant movement it can decrease or be disrupted if the spin of one or other chakra is compromised. We feel this as being out of sorts in various ways, physically or emotionally, and certain areas of our lives seem unbalanced. Each chakra corresponds to a particular area of the physical body (in medical terms, they seem to be closely associated with the endocrine system), and our physical and emotional health is affected if chakras are blocked, depleted or over-stimulated.

The Eastern cultural view is that what we do and how we behave is affected by this movement of energy around the body. So the chakras are essential to our connection to the universe and our own higher consciousness; when energy is flowing freely, we can achieve optimal levels of physical, emotional, mental and spiritual wellbeing.

The first time I experienced a chakra clearing session myself, I agreed to it mainly to be polite – a friend offered and I didn't like to say "No". Besides, it was free so I had nothing to lose, did I? I didn't realise how much I would actually gain from that first session though; not only did I feel happier and lighter afterwards, I began to understand better how energy works.

Visualising the chakras as invisible wheels helps us to become aware of the energy flow through our bodies. My friend Daisy encouraged me to see the spinning chakras like an old-fashioned barber's pole, gradually appearing to increase in length as each centre was activated. Then, once everything was in harmony, I slowed the pole down until we were back to where we started.

Before and after the visualisation, Daisy's method of checking the energy was to use a pendulum. She explained that the energy in the lower three 'physical' chakras is more likely to be stuck and the pendulum hardly moves, whereas the four higher are more connected to our 'spiritual' being and the pendulum is usually more active. After the session, neither of us could believe the difference in energy flow: the pendulum was swinging around like a fairground ride. Another friend who was with me confirmed the result, using the pendulum to check it was moving of its own accord with no external help.

Naturally, each healer has their own way of working. For myself, I like my client to work with me if possible, so I guide them through a visualisation – seeing the chakras as coloured flowers opening one petal at a time – as I hover my palms over each position in turn and allow the universal energy to flow freely through them. Before we end, we close the petals of each flower in turn. Some clients feel the energy shifts for themselves, there may be tingling feelings, warmth or coldness, but it's quite normal to feel nothing at first. There is always a sense of deep relaxation afterwards.

Chakra balancing is a way of ensuring that the body's subtle energy system is in good health, restoring harmony where the stresses of life have disrupted the flow. It can also reveal significant conditions that someone has been unaware of or unconsciously suppressing.

Jack is a healer who shared with me the story of a lady who had come to him with anxiety issues some months after losing her mother suddenly in an accident. Maureen was grieving, of course, but also experiencing panic attacks and sleeplessness, and didn't understand why. When she arrived for her session she was very tearful and it was some time before she was calm enough to begin. Unsurprisingly, Jack found the heart chakra, where we most feel the emotion of grief, to be out of balance and in need of healing.

However, he also soon noticed that the root chakra was 'stuck' and severely depleted of energy, suggesting that Maureen may be holding on to feelings of fear and anger.

There's a normal correlation between all these emotions, especially when someone passes suddenly and unexpectedly, as in this case. Jack focused his healing on these chakras and then invited Maureen, who immediately felt far more relaxed, to consider what he had found. She admitted for the first time openly that, yes, she had a deep fear of facing life alone without her mother. She also agreed, although not so easily, that she often felt there was a great injustice in the circumstances of her mother's passing.

All these emotions had overwhelmed Maureen and had manifested in anxiety, panic attacks and insomnia. The stress hormone cortisol is released in times of stress, a primitive link back to our survival instincts and thus the root chakra, and an overload of cortisol in continued stress will manifest in the symptoms Maureen was experiencing. It's a fact that in the aftermath of loved ones' passing there are higher than normal hospital admissions with suspected heart or severe anxiety attacks. The medical profession calls this Broken Heart Syndrome; it's not something one can 'just get over', there needs to be understanding of why it's happening and how to deal with it before it escalates into a critical physical issue.

After Jack's healing, Maureen reported that she'd had her best night's sleep for months and this continued over the next few weeks. She then returned for a second chakra clearing because she instinctively felt it was necessary if she were to heal fully and put her anxieties behind her for good. Jack remarked on the improvement in her energy flow, although he did sense that the root chakra was beginning to deplete again, which was why Maureen had realised she needed a follow-up appointment.

Very interestingly, during this second session and afterwards, she began to feel a connection with her mother's energy for the first time since her passing, sensing her presence around her. A little later, Maureen's mother also made contact with a message for her daughter at a demonstration of mediumship; that couldn't have happened while Maureen was so weighed down with grief, fear and anxiety.

The Seven Major Chakras

✳ Base or Root

Located at the base of the spine, this chakra's symbol is a lotus flower with four petals. Its Sanskrit name is Muladhara, meaning root, and it serves as our connection to the Earth and our basic survival instincts. It's associated with the colour red.

If this chakra is blocked, we may feel ungrounded or 'spaced out', and we may not care for ourselves physically as well as we should, becoming weak or fearful as a result. An overactive root chakra, though, could mean we're too attached to material life and physical possessions.

Physically, it's linked to the lower body, skeleton, blood, adrenal glands and teeth.

❋ Sacral

In the lower abdomen below the navel, the sacral chakra governs creativity, sexuality and reproduction. Represented by a six-petal lotus, it's Sanskrit name is Svadhisthana, meaning 'sweeten'. Its colour is orange.

This is the joy chakra and if its energy is depleted we may be denying our desires. If it's heightened, we could be too focused on physical pleasures and unwilling to acknowledge that these may not be in our best interests.

The sacral governs the reproductive and urinary waste disposal systems located in the lower abdomen.

❋ Solar Plexus

Represented by a ten-petal lotus, this chakra is just below the ribs and thought of as yellow in colour. Its Sanskrit name is Manipura and it's associated with our willpower, responsibility and self-confidence.

If it's off balance, we can be oversensitive to the opinions of others and self-critical, whilst an overactive solar plexus can make us forceful and over-confident.

The solar plexus chakra is linked to the digestive system and the pancreas, gall bladder, liver and spleen.

✳ Heart

In the middle of the chest, the fourth chakra is green with the Sanskrit name Anahata. It can be visualised as a twelve-petal lotus and is linked to unconditional love.

In balance, the heart chakra gives us feelings of inner peace but, if we are too giving with little consideration for our own needs, it's probably overactive. If we lack empathy or compassion for others, the heart chakra may be depleted, and either way we could experience relationship issues.

The heart chakra is physically associated with the heart, lungs, breasts and circulatory system.

✳ Throat

The Sanskrit name of the throat chakra, located at the base of the neck, is Visuddha. It's visualised as blue and represented by a sixteen-petal lotus.

Associated with communication and 'speaking your truth', it's also thought to be the chakra of telepathy. When it is in balance, communication flows easily and with consideration for the feelings of others. If it's working too hard, we may become too verbal, meaning we're not listening to others; communication is a two-way thing after all. A sluggish throat chakra can make us uncommunicative, or we could be sending 'the wrong messages' to others.

It's linked to the thyroid, throat, neck and jaw area.

✳ Third Eye or Brow

Called Ajna in Sanskrit and situated between the eyebrows, the third eye is an indigo colour and is represented by a two-petal lotus.

It's the seat of our psychic senses and developing this chakra can help with clairvoyance, intuition, and sensing information and messages from Spirit. If it's overactive we're likely to be ungrounded, whereas low energy here can lead to 'tunnel vision' – the opposite of the open mind and heart we are aiming for when developing our psychic senses.

The third eye chakra is physically associated with the face, sinuses, eyes and pituitary gland.

❇ Crown

At the top of the head and represented by a lotus with no less than a thousand petals, the crown chakra is the seat of our connection to the divine. Called Sahasrara in Sanskrit, it's thought of as violet in colour and is the gateway for energy to enter our bodies.

If the crown chakra is overactive, we may be addicted to spiritual matters to the exclusion of other things, whilst a depletion of energy leaves us bored and restless. When it's in good flow, we feel balanced in mind, body and spirit, and closer to our higher self.

The crown chakra is linked to the pineal gland, skull and brain.

Whilst most healers will focus on these seven major chakras, there are many more spread through the physical body, some say well over a hundred. There are further chakras within the aura, outside the body. The Earth Star, around thirty centimetres below the feet, grounds us into the energy of the Earth and is our connection with the universe, keeping us in the moment. Then we have the Causal, Soul Star and Stellar Gateway chakras, around ten, fifteen and thirty centimetres above the head respectively. The Stellar Gateway enables our connection with the divine, whilst the Causal and Soul Star help to deepen our spiritual connection and wisdom. Learning about the chakra system can be a helpful link to other areas of spirituality too, since it incorporates a number of different disciplines.

Some practitioners, like Daisy, like to use a pendulum as a visible demonstration of chakra wellness, but traditionally there was no requirement for pendulums, crystals or other external divination tools in healing work, just as the colour associations were only introduced in modern times. On the other hand, these may help to understand the system and deepen one's spiritual knowledge.

It's the result that matters, of course. After my own first session, I felt relaxed and more positive about everything even though it was at a time when my marriage was crumbling around me as Ted's illness turned him into a stranger. The healing helped me to stay calm and the feelings of hopelessness and depression that were my constant companions at that time dissipated. For the first time in ages, I felt I could cope. And that day set me on the path of learning as much as possible about using energy work as a means of helping myself and others to heal on all levels.

As we have seen, chakra clearing is always very relaxing. However, Alan was an insomniac, a self-confessed worrier who tended to go over the events of the day like a pathologist at a postmortem, examining everything even when things had been going well. Of course, when we do that we can always find things to worry about, which robs us of good sleep. He'd tried everything including herbal remedies but nothing seemed to help. I suggested a chakra clearing and healing session, and he was at the stage where he was willing to try anything even though he was pretty sceptical.

My intention was to pay particular attention to the crown chakra; physically, this governs the pineal gland that regulates sleep patterns. He came in the early evening so the treatment would have the best chance of helping him, all the day's stresses being out of the way, and I explained that anything we could do to boost the crown chakra should help him establish a sleep routine.

Naturally, it would be important for Alan to be fully relaxed and feeling good about himself when he went to bed. He was familiar with the usual advice about keeping the bedroom dark and free of electronic devices such as mobile phones, and I made two further suggestions. Firstly, he should focus on his breathing when he went to bed, with a cycle of three breaths in, held for a count of three before exhaling, then gradually increasing the number of breaths in each cycle for as long as he felt comfortable.

I also suggested he might use a simple affirmation, expressed as a thought rather than spoken aloud, to help clear his mind so the body could rest. Many energy healers believe that sincere affirmations can help to rewire the unconscious mind and change our thought patterns; this is especially effective alongside chakra healing if the affirmations are geared to particular chakras. The affirmation had to be something Alan could believe in, rather than just repeating it by rote. So because the crown is about feeling that all is right in our world and Alan said he just wanted to be at peace, without dissecting every event of the day, we settled on the simple sentence:

"I am at peace and all is well with my world."

He left the session feeling relaxed and motivated to deal with his insomnia. That night, still relaxed from the chakra clearing session, he had no trouble going to sleep but woke up after a few hours. He did the breathing exercises, then switched to the affirmation and soon found himself drifting off and staying asleep until the morning. It was, he told me, the best night's sleep he could ever remember. Going forward, chakra healing with focus on the crown, combined with the breathing and affirmation, helped him manage his insomnia rather than being a slave to it.

A Chakra Clearing Visualisation

Allow plenty of time when you won't be disturbed, take a bathroom break to be sure you are comfortable through the visualisation, and have a drink of water ready for when you finish. Lie down or sit in a comfortable place, take a few calming breaths and close the eyes.

❋ Visualise the root chakra as a wheel turning clockwise in a steady spin. If it helps, use the colour associations described earlier, starting here with red. When this is steady, do the same with the sacral chakra but keep the movement of the root chakra going too, so they spin in alignment.

✳ Repeat this process through all the chakras – solar plexus, heart, throat, third eye and crown – allowing thirty to sixty seconds for each one. Imagine that you are building a spinning pole, similar to an old-fashioned barber's pole, all the way up through the torso.

✳ Once all seven wheels are steadily spinning in alignment, slow down the movement and then reverse the spin so that the chakras now turn anticlockwise.

✳ Slow down the movement again until the wheels are no longer spinning and your body feels normal. Open the eyes and take a drink of water to help ground yourself. Experienced healers often report that, as the chakras clear and energy flow is restored, their clients may cough, sneeze or even cry; this is quite natural, a form of release.

If you wish, you may like to check your energy levels before and after the visualisation by holding a pendulum above each chakra in turn, working up from the root to the crown. If there is a block the pendulum will hardly move, but if energy is flowing freely it will swing around in a circle. Hopefully you will see a marked improvement afterwards and you will feel relaxed and lighter so repeat this visualisation whenever you feel your energy needs help to flow more freely.

Martin had a full-on coughing fit one day as I was working around his throat chakra. We'd been chatting for a while before starting and there had been no coughing then or earlier in the work. Once I moved past the throat chakra, it subsided as quickly as it had started. Now, coughing was mentioned above but this was at a specific point and during the session.

When the session was over, Martin confirmed that there was no physical cause for what happened, in fact he couldn't remember the last time he had coughed at all, let alone for more than a second or two. So I asked him whether he had any communication issues since the throat chakra is associated with 'speaking our truth'. Indeed, he was dreading having to tell his boss, George, that he was thinking of leaving to find a less stressful job. He felt disloyal as George was very supportive, but stress was making him depressed and he no longer enjoyed his work. Martin was impressed that this had shown up in his energy – he hadn't mentioned it to me or anyone else before now – and realised that it was affecting him deeply.

He resolved to have the conversation he'd been avoiding. Happily, once he expressed his thoughts, George was very understanding and rearranged Martin's workload to be less burdensome. He acknowledged that he'd been asking Martin to take on extra tasks occasionally and hadn't realised that this had got to the point where Martin felt he wasn't doing the job he'd originally been engaged for. Once the work was distributed more evenly, Martin was happy to stay where he was and began to enjoy his work again.

This was a case showing that working with the chakras can help us become more self-aware, recognising issues that could be affecting our life energy. Therefore, as we learn more about how the system works, we may choose to work with chakras individually; we may even benefit by wearing clothes or eating foods that correspond to the colours of particular chakras. Feeling anxious or lacking confidence? Try wearing red on the lower half of the body near the root chakra, and include red foods like tomatoes in your diet. Sore throat or difficulty communicating? Throw on a blue scarf and wear a tee-shirt or blouse with blue in it, and enjoy a blueberry smoothie.

To be fair, there is as yet no scientific evidence that such strategies have a real effect, although there is considerable anecdotal evidence to support the theory of colours. Quite a few people make their colour choices based on how they feel and what they need to accomplish on a certain day. For example, if there's a potentially difficult meeting planned with someone who can be quick to anger, one might wear blue. This sets the intention of staying calm and communicating particularly well to avoid possible triggers; with any luck, the colour will also have a calming influence on the other person! Is this chakra colours or psychology? It could just be that one is putting more thought into the meeting, or perhaps the blue is working with the throat chakra, we can't be sure. But if it seems to work, let's keep our minds and options open.

Another example of chakra clearing leading to greater self-awareness as well as healing came when Eve received a session as a gift. She didn't know much in advance about the energy system and certainly didn't expect to find relief from the knee pain that had plagued her for months.

During the session, her therapist reported that Eve's root chakra seemed blocked so afterwards she asked whether Eve had any family issues: perhaps she felt that she was the one carrying the troubles of her family without much support? This was spot on, Eve agreed. She was caring for her mother who was in the early stages of dementia and had recently come to live with them after the sudden death of Eve's father. At the same time, her grown-up daughter was going through a difficult divorce and was calling Eve at all hours to talk about her problems. Eve literally felt that she was carrying the weight of the world on her shoulders.

Feeling 'put upon' emotionally, especially in family matters, can often result in physical pain in the legs as they are governed by the root chakra. Talking through her emotional worries enabled Eve to make the connection with her knee pain, which had come out of the blue and was not connected to any other health conditions. She also realised that she needed to set boundaries and get help to cope with her family so she engaged a part-time carer for her mother, arranged counselling for her daughter, and asked her husband to help more around the house.

Eve had been used to running the household with no issues, but once things started to go wrong she hadn't realised how much everything had overwhelmed her until her therapist identified the blockage of her energy and explained how personal issues can manifest physically. Who would have thought that knee pain could originate from taking on the troubles of the family? Then again, the knees are load-bearing joints. Within a couple of weeks of that session, Eve's knee pain was easier and after a month it had completely cleared up.

Learning about the chakras can help us understand the mind-body-spirit connection and make us more aware of our own energy on different levels. Then we can be more proactive and empowered in how we use our energy, knowing how the various areas of the body work and how we can help to keep them healthy.

A Visualisation to Clear the Mind

Sometimes there's so much chatter in our heads that we can't seem to do anything to stop it. It keeps us awake at night, stops us from concentrating on the task in hand and makes us anxious. This is a simple visualisation to 'empty the head' and enjoy being in the moment. It's a good exercise to do at any time but particularly helpful if we have trouble sleeping at night.

* Sit or lie down comfortably, relax the body by slow breathing and close the eyes.

* Visualise the inside of your head full of boxes (for our purposes, the brain has left the building!). Some people like to imagine climbing up into the attic of their home, where all kinds of 'stuff' has been dumped in boxes.

* Observe the boxes carefully. How many are there? What shape and colour are they? Are they large or small?

* Don't open any of the boxes. We don't need to know what's inside them. Instead, visualise yourself collecting them up one by one and removing them from your head (or attic). Make a pile of them on the floor, out of your line of vision, although you know it's there.

* When the last box has been moved, look around at the clear space left behind. Enjoy being there in the peace and quiet where no thoughts or worries intrude. Spend as long as you like just contemplating the space you have created.

* When you feel ready, open your eyes and come back to the room. There's no need to return the boxes to your head space – they

represent temporary thoughts and impressions and they will fade away of their own accord.

CHAPTER SEVEN

Healing Crystals

Do you think of crystals as pretty pieces of jewellery or as decorations for the house, or do you see them as powerful containers and transmitters of energy? I was firmly in the first camp until I saw results when working with healing crystals that defied logical explanation. This is a subject that can take some getting used to for some people yet I've become convinced that it can be another great way to tap into the energy of the universe and to learn more about ourselves and how our energy, er, rocks!

There's no validated evidence as yet to support crystal healing; scientists say that, other than a minor electrical charge in crystals that may result in slight changes of the body's energetic flow, there are no measurable healing benefits in working with them. On the other hand, many experts agree that there seems to be at least a certain placebo effect when working with crystals, inducing relaxation, reducing stress and encouraging a sense of wellbeing. Then again, the same can be said for a lot of psychic and spiritual work. There are innumerable stories in different areas of energy work that seem to defy rational explanation (and it is clear that we don't yet understand whatever subtle energy is involved).

There is an interesting argument for the placebo effect in a book by Roland Rotherham about holy wells, the Celtic saints of Cornwall and the legend of King Arthur.[1] Discussing what makes particular waters 'holy' in the minds of spiritual seekers, the author writes:

'Some may feel baptismal cleansing and rebirth might be a palliative effect... but this allows the divine spark to be released... [P]lacebo or not, it is seen to exist and therefore flourishes... Any form of spiritual exercise must by its very nature be interactive.'

Perhaps this argument applies equally to the use of crystals and, indeed, to many other things that can't be explained by science yet seem to be of benefit in ways we don't yet understand. When people believe that something works and spread the word about it – say, an alternative therapy – this attracts others who also come to believe, either through their own experience or from seeing the evidence in others. The same can be said for crystals. When healers report genuinely good results with the use of certain crystals, others will then use them and trust in their energy.

However, there are many anecdotal accounts by spiritually sensitive people of being strongly drawn to certain crystals and feeling a powerful energy that makes a difference in the way they or their clients feel. They may be more relaxed, sleep better, become less prone to temper or anxiety, and there may be genuine physical healing too. These people will affirm that certain crystals have definite healing properties.

I was invited to a friend's birthday party and had no idea what to take as a gift. Guy was depressed because his relationship had hit a rocky patch, so I chose a beautiful piece of black tourmaline; it would make a nice feature and, I hoped, dispel the negativity around their home. Guy placed it in their bedroom and almost immediately, he reported later, he and his partner began to sleep better and argue less. After a couple of weeks, they were both feeling more positive and their relationship was back on track.

Tourmaline is renowned for helping us to be more grounded and relaxed, able to see a situation in a new light and feel encouraged to make a few necessary changes. In any case, Guy has kept the piece close ever

---

[1] *Sacred Falls: Saint Nectan and the Legacy of the Dragon* (St Nectan's Waterfall Publications, 2014)

since and life is still good for the couple. Interestingly, Guy believes in crystal power but his partner doesn't, yet both benefited from the crystal.

In the previous chapter we saw that some healers believe there to be correspondences between the chakras and crystals, so let's look at the ones that are commonly used, and why.

Root or base chakra

Red in colour, this chakra is concerned with basic physical needs, grounding and stability so it is associated with red or black crystals such as black tourmaline, said to protect against negative energies and also our own negative thoughts.

Haematite is also associated with the root chakra, as a grounding stone that helps with the mind-body connection.

Red jasper is another powerful crystal, known as 'the stone of endurance' because warriors used to carry it on the battlefield to give them strength and courage. In Norse legend, Siegfried the Dragon Slayer carried a sword inlaid with red jasper to bring him courage.

Sacral

This energy centre is thought of as orange, so stones such as carnelian and orange calcite work here. Carnelian is named from the Latin word for 'flesh'. The ancient Egyptians believed it was helpful for the menstrual cycle and, since the sacral is connected to the reproductive system, we can see why carnelian has been used.

Orange calcite is also said to have healing properties for the sexual organs, as well as helping to heal emotional issues associated with sexuality and infertility.

Solar plexus

This chakra is related to our self-esteem so many healers use citrine, the yellow stone of abundance, here. Abundance is not just about financial and material gain (although citrine can help with that too). If one lacks confidence and self-worth, the joy of life depleted, then having citrine in the home or wearing jewellery made from citrine can really boost one's mood and increase motivation.

Yellow jasper is also helpful, a nurturing stone that can help with digestive disorders such as heartburn and eating disorders, as well as giving confidence a boost.

Heart

Pink and green are both associated with the heart, green representing the physical aspects of the heart, such as the circulation and blood pressure, and pink the emotional aspects of love, grief and loss. A favourite stone used here is the beautiful green aventurine, often called 'the lucky stone', whose name comes from the Italian word for 'chance'. It helps to regulate energy and soothe anxiety, so it works on both the physical and emotional aspects of the heart.

Then of course there is rose quartz, 'the love stone'. This crystal has a gentle calming energy and helps foster compassion and kindness as well as reducing anger. Many people like to keep rose quartz in the bedroom as they feel its gentle energy helps them sleep.

Throat

The throat chakra is all about communication, and is thought of as blue. Sodalite may be unfamiliar to some as it was only discovered in the nineteenth century. It looks a bit like the sea on a stormy day, being flecked with white calcite, and it's linked to all aspects of communication as well as physical healing for the throat. Also known as 'the poets' stone', it's said to enhance creativity and help us to find the right words, whether written or spoken.

We can also use turquoise here, one of the first gemstones to be mined about six thousand years ago. The ancient Egyptians buried turquoise in the tombs of their dead to accompany them to the afterlife, and these days it is also thought to help with divine communication and spiritual insight.

Third Eye

Related to spiritual insight and clairvoyance, this chakra's colour is indigo, a deep shade of blue, although some healers prefer to use purple stones here since it is a colour traditionally associated with spirituality. A good first choice of crystal here is amethyst for its gentle, calming energy that encourages serenity and a state of acceptance, ready to receive spiritual guidance and insights. Amethyst is also thought to enhance natural psychic abilities.

Another good stone for the third eye is blue labradorite. An iridescent, deep blue stone, it helps us see the bigger picture as well as protecting us from negative energy as we develop our psychic powers.

Crown

Our connection to the divine and to the world of Spirit beyond our understanding, its colours are violet or white and many healers use clear quartz when working with the crown chakra. Clear quartz is also called the 'master healer'; not only can it alleviate any physical or emotional issues, it's a powerful energy amplifier so, when used with other crystals, it magnifies their properties. It's particularly associated with spiritual growth.

Amethyst can also be used with the crown, or another white stone is selenite. Named for the moon goddess, Selene, it is said to facilitate contact with the spirit world and with angels by promoting calmness, clarity and the clear flow of energy.

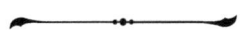

When I adopted my rescue dog, Luna, my friends Stuart and his wife Adele came round to meet her but I noticed immediately that Stuart wasn't his normal, laid-back self. He was not 'in the moment' and he couldn't relax (even after a couple of glasses of wine!). Adele explained that he was going through a very stressful time in his professional life. He was running a successful business but the workload was particularly heavy and there had been issues with his business partner, resulting in a parting of the ways.

I had recently discovered a relaxation technique using selenite and felt sure it would help Stuart to destress and enjoy his down time. Selenite has a lovely gentle, calming energy, and whilst all crystals are beneficial in different ways I believe that selenite is special, one of the best crystals for transmuting negative energy and removing fearful thoughts.

Stuart removed his shoes and placed his feet on a selenite wand, then I guided him to focus on deep breathing until he felt fully relaxed: breathing in the shimmering white healing light of the selenite for a count of three, holding the breath for three, then breathing out his stress for a count of three. The exhales were assigned a dark colour and he was to visualise them becoming paler with each breath until he was breathing out clear, colourless air, signifying that the tension had left his body.

After a few minutes, Stuart was in deep relaxation with his head drooping forward and he wasn't coming back to us yet. When Luna came charging in, landing her front paws on Stuart's stockinged feet, I was concerned that the shock of the Luna Landing would undo all the good work that the breathing and selenite had brought about. However, even twenty-five kilos of excited dog didn't affect him!

About fifteen minutes later, Stuart came back to the room gently and naturally, with no recollection of Luna bouncing over him. The good news is that the destress session worked and, with the techniques I talked him through that evening and using his own selenite wand, he's been able to manage his own stress levels since then. Crystals may not be essential components of energy work, but they do help to focus the mind on what we want to achieve and they can also help raise the vibrations around us.

When I give card readings at spiritual fairs and the like, I offer each client a small crystal to take away with them. Invariably, I know which crystal they will choose, depending on how the reading has unfolded. If someone needs more serenity and less drama in their life, they will usually choose amethyst or rose quartz; if they are struggling to communicate their feelings clearly, it will probably be sodalite. It seems that the crystal 'speaks' to where the person needs physical or emotional healing.

Just as many believe there to be a link between crystals and the chakras, there's certainly a correspondence between their colours and the areas of our lives we need to heal. After all, certain stones were considered to have particular healing properties long before they were associated with the chakras. So if you are drawn to certain crystal colours, apart from their obvious aesthetic attractions, they may be suggesting that there's an issue to be looked at.

The ones described here are easy-to-come-by but there are several specialised books for deeper study, such as those by Judy Hall.[2]

Red

Red crystals help to boost our metabolism, stoke up our enthusiasm and restore passion and motivation with increased confidence and strength. Red aventurine and red agate are the best here, whilst garnet is good for calming anxiety and helping us deal with fears and phobias. Most red stones also promote physical healing in the legs and feet, hips and adrenal glands.

Orange

These crystals are believed to help us find our joy and confidence, as well as healing issues related to the bladder or reproductive system. The beautiful orange agate is an excellent grounding stone that promotes courage and orange aventurine is another powerhouse crystal that fires

---

[2] *The Crystal Bible* (3 Volumes, Godsfield Press, 2019)

the imagination and optimism in aiming for what the soul desires. Sunstone brings warmth and light into the chill of winter and helps those affected by Seasonal Affective Disorder; it is also thought to ease joint pain and boost the metabolism.

Yellow

Spiritually speaking, yellow is often seen as the colour of abundance and joy, and yellow stones can give our energy a boost, especially yellow agate. Yellow calcite offers gentle support when our self-esteem is low and helps us see clearly why certain patterns don't serve our best interests, whilst topaz can help us attract the right people into our lives.

Green

Although all crystals are said to have healing properties, green is the colour most people associated with physical and emotional healing because it's a predominant and calming colour in nature. Jade is particularly linked to healing for the kidneys and bladder, and to regulating the body's fluid levels. Alternatively, malachite is a stone of protection, keeping negative energies at bay with its powerful energy, so it's not a stone to keep by the bedside. If you want a stone to help with divine connection, try a small piece of moldavite.

Blue

Blue is the colour of the oceans and the sky, so it's soothing and calming for the body and the soul. Lapis lazuli is a beautiful ancient stone, beloved of the Egyptians and ground into a pigment by Michelangelo for the painting of the Sistine Chapel. Physically, it's said to boost the immune system, heal the thyroid and throat and help with insomnia and depression. Aquamarine encourages us to go with the flow, whilst blue quartz helps us communicate better with the higher self by boosting our intuition.

Purple

Purple is the colour most people associate with spiritual life, and charoite (sometimes confused with amethyst as they are very similar in appearance) is said to be excellent for boosting our connection with the spirit world. On the physical level, purple stones can help to ease headaches and depression. Purple fluorite is a beautiful stone that can bring relief from arthritic pain, and as a bonus it also keeps negative energies at bay.

Black

Black crystals help with grounding, protection and keeping negativity at bay. A favourite is black tourmaline but there's also obsidian, which can help us step away from bad habits and bring more balance to our lives. Onyx is helpful for healing old wounds and dealing with overwhelm; indeed, black stones in general can give us much comfort.

Brown

With the colours of the Earth, brown crystals are mainly used for grounding and balance. Tiger's eye is both very beautiful and good for dealing with physical exhaustion and calming anger. Smoky quartz is classed as a brown stone, although when tumbled it can appear more like a cloudy quartz; it's another crystal that keeps us grounded when dealing with practical matters and helps to transmute negative thoughts.

Pink

Many people would think of rose quartz here, but there's also pink tour-maline; it often grows through clear quartz, giving the dual benefit of the master healer and a stone that promotes kindness and acceptance. Rhodochrosite is a stunning, banded pink stone that is said to heal the heart emotionally and physically. All pink stones have a gentle, soothing energy and are the ones to choose for any issue related to the blood.

Clear or white

Like purple stones, white or clear crystals are mainly used to enhance our psychic gifts and strengthen our spiritual connection. As well as clear quartz and selenite, already mentioned, howlite is a great calming stone that can strengthen connection with the angelic realm. It is also said to balance calcium levels and strengthen the bones, teeth and hair. Moonstone is usually associated with feminine energy, helping with issues around fertility and menstruation, but it can help anyone with the emotions of change and transformation.

All of these crystals are renowned for their specific healing properties and most of them are readily available and reasonably priced, although moldavite is less easy to find. How do we choose the crystals to work with? Well, we can do some research and ask the owners of New Age shops for guidance, but many people find that the crystals will choose us! There seems to be a certain attraction at work that draws us to the crystals we need at particular stages of our lives.

Barbara was looking at crystal bracelets on my stall and was strongly attracted to a purple fluorite piece. As mentioned, this is said to be very helpful for arthritic joint pain and for balance problems. Barbara was indeed having real difficulty with her right hip and she also had a touch of vertigo, meaning she was often disorientated and in pain. She was drawn to the fluorite – or was it calling to her?

She bought the bracelet and when I saw her a few weeks later, her hip was much more comfortable and her vertigo had all but disappeared. She was convinced it was the fluorite that had brought about the transformation, and put it on each morning before getting out of bed. In time, she was still wearing the bracelet and still enjoying a mostly pain-free life. Purple fluorite is also a good calming stone that helps people relax, which is clearly beneficial for chronic pain.

I can also attest to the energy of purple fluorite for joint problems. I was having problems with the little finger on my right hand which was bent badly due to arthritis and, on this particular day, was hot and swollen. Tom, the owner of my favourite crystal shop, suggested I try a purple fluorite bracelet and wear it constantly for a few weeks. I followed his advice and, within a month, I noticed that the finger had straightened out somewhat; not only that, but the same finger on my left hand, which was also starting to bend out of shape, was virtually back to normal.

The improvement continued for some weeks until eventually the bracelet snapped and the stones scattered. I collected them up and took them back to Tom, asking him to repair the bracelet, but he said that the crystals were telling me I didn't need them any longer. To be honest, I was rather sceptical about that but several years down the line there has been no more pain or inflammation in my little fingers and they have not bent out of shape again. Did the fluorite accomplish what my doctor said could only be corrected with surgery?

I met Gina at a spiritual circle and we got talking about crystals and their uses. She told me that she was troubled with vertigo, and I suggested that rose quartz can help with physical and emotional balance. I had a small piece of rose quartz in my pocket and gave it to her to try, advising her to carry it with her all day and to sleep with it under her pillow. The following week, she reported that her vertigo had almost completely disappeared.

But then a few weeks later, her symptoms returned and she couldn't understand why. She checked her pockets and discovered the stone was missing from its usual place. At the time, her husband was away on business and when he returned he gave her back the rose quartz, which he'd found on the bedroom floor the morning he left and had slipped into his pocket. He had intended to give it back to her on the way to the airport but forgot all about it. Once Gina's rose quartz was back where it belonged, the vertigo was soon under control again, although she did buy another stone so she would never be without one again!

Personal experiences with black tourmaline in particular have convinced me there's much more to crystal power than a placebo effect. This stone is said to protect our energy and the space around us, preventing negative energy from entering our home. Some even recommend walking around the perimeter of the home periodically while holding a piece, to cleanse and bless the home and everyone who enters it. I keep a piece of natural tourmaline by my front door.

During the difficult times with my husband, I wore a black tourmaline bracelet constantly, again on Tom's advice. Even on the night Paddy died, the bracelet stayed intact despite the struggles with my dog and with Ted. However, a few weeks later when I had separated from Ted and returned to our Spanish home for a while to recover, I was standing quietly in the middle of the living room and the bracelet just fell away from my wrist, scattering beads all over the floor.

I sensed that I no longer needed protection from Ted's energy and that he would never return to Spain; indeed, I felt certain we would never meet again. As the thought passed through my mind, Ted's favourite cuckoo clock just fell from the wall and shattered on the floor as though to confirm my gut feelings. Synchronicities like these are powerful evidence of spiritual energy.

Soon after this, back in the UK and staying with my friend Gill, she told me she was having problems with her next door neighbours. It had started with loud music that they refused to turn down and then escalated over a few weeks to the point when the police had to be called as she was being physically threatened and verbally abused. Gill was even considering moving and was using the side door to minimise any encounters with the neighbours.

Remembering my own experience, I bought a big piece of tourmaline and blessed the house, asking that the peace and tranquility that had attracted Gill in the first place be restored so she could enjoy her home again. I then placed the stone alongside the party wall.

Within a week, we noticed that things were calmer next door and we heard that the woman had moved out and left her partner. He even called round to apologise for their behaviour and explained that his partner had been having emotional difficulties. A few weeks later they reconciled and we braced ourselves for a resumption of hostilities: it didn't happen and harmony was restored on the street.

Something had changed the dynamic in that household for the better. Was it the tourmaline? Some may well be sceptical but several other experiences have led me to believe that black tourmaline is a very special stone.

The world of crystals can seem daunting at first, with the sheer number of them and different varieties of the same stones (there are lots of different agates, for example). But if we first learn about the general properties for the stones we are particularly drawn to, by visiting websites or talking to people like Tom, they soon become easier to understand.

Take agate, for example, a wonderful balancing stone that comes in several different colours. Its basic property is to harmonise masculine and feminine energies and balance the physical, emotional and intellectual aspects of the body. Yet it's also said to help strengthen the immune system, boost the metabolism, stabilise blood pressure and assist cell repair and renewal. It helps us let go of the past and accept change rather than resisting it.

In particular, blue agate can help with communication, red agate gives us courage and strengthens our will, and black agate is grounding, helping to calm anger and dispel negativity. All varieties of this powerful crystal, however, will have the core properties of harmony and balance.

Crystals are sold in various forms and, again, we should just go with whatever speaks to us or seems most attractive. They can be raw or natural, straight from the Earth, tumbled to give them a shiny appearance, or sculpted into shapes such as pyramids, skulls, angels, animals or wands. Then there are geodes (from the Greek *geoides*, meaning Earth-like), from the fairly small to the enormous, which are said to direct positive energy flow in the home. The outer casing of a geode is unremarkable, looking like any rock, but inside they are hollowed out with many crystalline points, formed over millions of years.

We should let instinct and budget guide us when choosing crystals to work with. Their size does not determine the strength of their energy, and polishing or shaping crystals doesn't detract from their healing properties, although those with points or in pyramid shapes are believed by some to concentrate and amplify energy.

A final word of caution here though… Collecting crystals can become addictive as, whatever their healing properties, they are such beautiful things. There's no point in spending a fortune on calming crystals, then becoming stressed about where the money for our bills is coming from!

CHAPTER EIGHT

Who Are the Angels?

Erica lived with her son David, although they didn't see a lot of each other because they worked different shifts. One evening he was invited out by friends after work, which was a regular thing to do, but this time he decided to go home and share his evening meal with his mother. His friends weren't impressed as he'd originally agreed to join them, but he couldn't be persuaded. While Erica was cooking, she suddenly collapsed. She begged him not to call an ambulance because she worked as a paramedic and hated the thought of her colleagues being called out unnecessarily. Fortunately, David insisted because it transpired that Erica was having a brain stem stroke.

For two weeks her life hung in the balance and her doctors told her she wouldn't have survived if David hadn't been at home to call the ambulance. On the same night, there were two other brain stem stroke admissions to the same hospital and neither patient survived. Erica is convinced it was a guardian angel who persuaded her son to turn down the invitation to a night out, a very unusual decision for him.

Ten years on, Erica is still working as a paramedic although the stroke left her with deafness in one ear and no control over her appetite centre. She never gets hungry and she never feels full; when David took her to an all-you-can-eat Chinese buffet to celebrate her recovery she went back to the buffet seven times! Her recovery was so remarkable, her consultant said he had never seen anything like it in thirty years of practice.

It certainly seemed like a miracle happened that evening. There are many accounts like this of people making life-changing decisions without having the faintest idea why, or even of a stranger on the street saving someone from great danger but then apparently vanishing. There is a growing interest and belief in angels now and, as more and more people turn to spirituality in order to make sense of their own issues and what is happening in the world, angels have emerged from myth and history and come back to our daily lives. Certainly, many of those involved in spiritual work, such as mediums and healers, believe strongly that they are helped by the angelic world.

Most of us will be familiar with religious stories about angels – there are frequent references in the Bible and the Qur'an – but perhaps see them as mythical or supernatural beings, rather anachronistic to the challenges of life here on Earth today. Yet an increasing number of people now think of them as our guides and friends, with whom we can build a relationship once we consciously call them into our lives.

So who are these rather special beings and how can they help us on our spiritual journeys? The term angel comes from the Greek *angelos*, meaning 'messenger', so essentially they are a bridge between Heaven and Earth, linking humanity to God, or Source or Spirit.

Various beliefs about angels have developed across time and different cultures, for example that they were created with free will but gave it up in order to serve God and protect humanity. Nowadays, most people think of them as without gender, although traditionally it's been human nature to think of certain angels as male and others as female. In the Bible and other religious texts, they are usually referred to as masculine but Archangel Gabriel, as the angel of motherhood, is today often thought of as female, as is Jophiel, the angel of beauty and wisdom. On the other hand, the angel of love and peace, Chamuel, won't mind if his pink ray means we assume he is feminine. Angels don't get offended, they are loving and non-judgemental beings.

They can appear in different ways to different people in different situations. Whilst traditionally they have been depicted in art with wings, they are beings of spirit and they don't have a physical body. Thus they can take on any shape they wish and may even present to us in human form, so as not to frighten us, or with wings since that is how we are conditioned to recognise them. Just as Heaven is still often referred to as 'up there', it has been natural to think of the inhabitants of a celestial world as beings with flight.

There are numerous descriptions of angels having wings in the Bible and other major sacred texts such as the Qur'an and the Talmud. Christianity, Islam and Judaism seem to agree that angels have wings.

'Above him were seraphim, each with six wings. With two they covered their faces, with two they covered their feet, and with two they were flying.' (Isaiah 6: 2)

Elsewhere in the Bible, wings are mentioned as symbolic of God's love and care, both His gift and a symbol of the magnificence of His creation.

'He will cover you with feathers, and under His wings you will find refuge. His faithfulness will be your shield and rampart.' (Psalm 91: 4)

The Qur'an also speaks of winged angels.

'All praise belongs to God, the maker of the Heavens and the Earth, who made the angel messengers with wings, two or three or four pairs.' (Surah Fatir 35: 1)

Still, we may sense their presence as energy, see it as a colour or as orbs of light, or we may feel a change in the temperature around us, a tingling in our bodies or a ringing in our ears. There are many ways in which angels are believed to appear to and communicate with us. Some people have reported the sensation of being hugged or held close, and there are even accounts of angels using technology to get our attention...

Caroline, one of our neighbours, was woken up randomly by a loud signal from her Amazon Alexa device at around four o'clock one winter morning. Both she and her husband Keith are 'tech savvy' and are certain there was nothing they had done that might have caused such a rude awakening. Being wide awake, though, Caroline reasoned that she may as well check on her four year-old daughter, Opal, who had been diagnosed with Type 1 diabetes. She found Opal very pale and sweating profusely, classic signs of hypoglycaemia, or dangerously low blood sugar levels.

Thankfully, they were able to deal with the situation quickly and Opal soon recovered, but things could have been very different if Alexa hadn't intervened. Caroline is convinced that this was a case of angelic intervention, that Opal's guardian angel had used Alexa to get her attention. When they had the device checked later that day, there was nothing wrong with it and nothing like this has ever happened since.

It is now widely believed that guardian angels are assigned to each of us before we incarnate on Earth and remain with us throughout our lives, perhaps accompanying us through more than one incarnation. Some say we have just one such guardian whilst many spiritual people feel it's more likely that we have a team, coming and going for different situations throughout our lives.

Despite so many biblical accounts of angels intervening and helping in the lives of men, the Christian Church has little to say about the afterlife or 'the ministry of angels'. This is something that greatly frustrated the twentieth century devout Christian mystic John Cotton, for example, who was blessed with the most extraordinary spiritual gifts of clairaudience, automatism, psychic art and healing. He believed that there are simply two classes of angel, those created by God and inhabiting the highest spiritual planes, and humans who have passed on and become guardians or spirit helpers. He was very well aware of his own team of artists, doctors and the like – whose identities he also knew – and that they were overseen by a guardian, Joseph, a member of The White Brotherhood of Evolved Souls.

An outsider to many in the Church, John's beliefs could be thought of as a kind of compromise between traditional religion and modern spirituality. And when challenged by the orthodox that he was treading dangerous ground, he would simply quote 1 Corinthians 12: 4-10:

"…to one is given by the Spirit… the gifts of healing… to another, discerning of spirits…"

Esotericists have long believed that there is a hierarchy within the angelic world which is divided into three spheres, containing nine choirs. These are the seraphim, cherubim, thrones, dominions, virtues, powers, principalities, archangels and angels. In practice, it's the latter two choirs in 'the lowest sphere' who interact with us. Archangels are the ones who watch over and manage our life here on Earth and they each have their own areas of expertise and wider responsibilities. For example, Michael is the angel of protection and justice, whilst also being the protector of the nation of Israel.

Archangels and their Responsibilities

Ariel   The angel of nature and manifestation
Chamuel   The angel of peace and love
Zadkiel   The angel of freedom, mercy and forgiveness
Gabriel   The angel of creativity, communication and
            motherhood
Raziel   The angel of mystery and understanding
Metatron   The angel of the presence and of spiritual power
Jophiel   The angel of truth and beauty
Jeremiel   The angel of forgiveness and life review, helping us to
            understand our choices and their consequences
Raguel   The angel of relationships and fairness
Azrael   The angel of transition and change
Uriel   The angel of light, intelligence and understanding
Sandalphon The angel of prayer and music

Thus when we have a particular difficulty in our lives, we may call upon the appropriate archangel for guidance; for example, if we are struggling to let go of the pain that others have caused us, we would turn to Jeremiel.

In the same way that New Age thinkers have assigned colours to the chakras, many people now like to associate astrological birth signs to the archangels as a way of helping us to learn more about particular angels and their correspondences. For the list above, these would be, respectively: Aries, Taurus, Gemini, Cancer, Leo, Virgo, Libra, Scorpio, Sagittarius, Capricorn, Aquarius and Pisces.

Now, there are many, many thousands of angels: 'Then I looked, and I heard the voice of many angels around the throne, and the living creatures and the elders, and the number of them was myriads of myriads, and thousands of thousands.' (Revelations 10: 11) We can never know them all, nor do we need to. The important thing is how we see our personal relationships with them.

The archangels are there for everyone and can be in several places at once, whereas guardian angels are assigned to us personally as our guides. The archangels, if you like, are on hand to advise our guardian angels and to filter down requests from the higher ranks in ways that we as humans can understand, whereas guardian angels are closer to us, our friends and protectors. Indeed, there are many accounts of people who believe their guardian angels have kept them safe, as well as tales by people who feel they have been helped by archangels. They cannot interfere with our free will, but there is much evidence that they can intervene on our behalf if they feel we are in danger or straying from our true path.

Shirley was driving on a quiet road on her housing estate when she rounded a corner only to see another car parked right on the bend. Sure that she was going into the back of it and facing serious injury, she froze with fear. Then suddenly the steering wheel spun out of her hands and the car was on the other side of the road, still in one piece. She insists that she didn't swerve the car herself, and it seemed impossible that that would have made any difference because she was so close to the other vehicle, yet her car did an incredible manoeuvre.

Shirley's angel appeared as 'an energy' yet there are many stories in reputable publications of angels coming to Earth in human form to help when needed. Fred was a sailor who went ashore to relax with crewmates, only to discover that their drinks had been spiked with drugs. Back on the ship, some of the men were hallucinating and being rowdy so Fred, a spiritual man, prayed for help as he realised that the effects could last for many hours and the men would get into trouble.

Another sailor, very tall and well-built, emerged from a nearby cabin and asked what was wrong. He helped Fred to round up the affected sailors and bring them to his cabin where he got the men to share their good experiences in the Navy, to take their minds off their current situation. Fred reports that the effects of the drugs on himself and his crewmates started to wear off quickly, then they all said goodnight to their new friend and returned to their beds.

Next morning, Fred went to thank the sailor for his help but the door was locked and, when he asked where the sailor was, he was told that the cabin hadn't been used for months. When Fred described him, nobody remembered having seen him before and they never saw him again. Fred is convinced he was an angel, because who else would have the power to counteract the effects of the drugs on a group of men in just a few minutes?

I have trained as a certified Angel Guide myself and I like to work with angelic energy for healing, chakra clearing and psychic work such as card reading. I am quite sure that the visualisations in this book have been given to me in meditation by angels. Every night before sleep and first thing each morning, I talk to them and invite them to support me in my work. Indeed, I can't imagine my life now without the presence of angels, yet a while ago I had real difficulty making a connection and began to wonder if I'd ever get really close to them.

Well, everything happens with divine timing and once the relationship began, like other aspects of the Soul Cave journey, it developed rapidly. I felt that Archangel Chamuel, the angel of peace and love, could help to smoothe my relationship with Ted. The crystal most associated with Chamuel is rose quartz so I bought a bracelet that I could wear all the time and another piece for my bedside cabinet. I did feel calmer with the crystals around me, not so quick to rise to the triggers when an argument loomed, and I saw pink behind my closed eyes whenever I connected with Chamuel. By concentrating on keeping calm, it became my reality most of the time and, so far, it may seem that I did that myself without angelic help. However, when things escalated, I am sure it was Chamuel who came to my aid.

Ted wanted a cuckoo clock for his birthday. He liked his clocks and we already had three cuckoo clocks on the walls plus a Westminster chiming clock. Instead, I bought a beautiful, and silent, mango wood clock from a local artisan centre. He seemed pleased with it at first but, as the day continued and he drank more, he told me he wished I hadn't bought him anything and when we went to lunch with friends he was trying to give the clock to them, which made everyone feel uncomfortable. Back home, he threatened to put my present in the bin.

I was exhausted and upset, so I went to a friend's house to wait until Ted got the rage out of his system and slept off the drink. Once there, I sobbed until I had no more tears left before falling into a troubled sleep. Yet when I woke up, it felt exactly like someone was holding me close and comforting me, although I was alone in the room. Then I heard the words, "Don't feed the drama, don't lose your temper." I have no idea where this came from, but when I opened my eyes the whole room had a rosy glow about it, even though it was a cold and dark January evening and there was no lighting in the room.

I resolved there and then that I would never again lose my temper, with Ted or anyone else. Archangel Chamuel was there for me at my lowest point, he gave me comfort and a coping mechanism when I most needed it. Several years on from that night, this previously volatile Gemini has still never lost her temper whatever the provocation, much to the astonishment of those who know me. When Ted became difficult, I would stay silent or leave the room, even leave the house for a while, to take the heat from the situation. Neither I nor Chamuel could change his behaviour but, in that moment of angelic help, I learned to change my own responses to him (and to others).

It wasn't always easy, but I learned that getting into an argument, losing our temper or going on the defensive, however justifiably, only ever increases the negative energy and there are never any winners in that situation. In fact, it can be really empowering, refusing to be drawn into other people's drama. Receive an incendiary message or someone makes a provocative statement? Ignore it, change the subject or turn and walk away.

This story highlights one of the differences between guardian angels and archangels. Guardian angels are essentially our protectors and advisers; they can intervene when necessary to keep us safe and we can turn to them for advice to help us keep to our true spiritual path and to calm our doubts and fears. Archangels can help us more with major shifts in our state of mind when we are at turning points in life, because they have responsibility for the deeper aspects of life. The guardian's job is to be with us day by day whereas archangels are the specialists who can be called upon when significant changes are necessary.

When we are at a really low ebb, feeling that we have lost our direction or just don't know what to do, we can call on the angels for help. It's surprising how many people say that they talk to their loved ones in the spirit world, even feel their presence around them, but never think of talking to angels. Do we assume they must have better things to do than spend time on our problems, like announcing big plans for the universe, because that's how they have usually been portrayed in religious writings? No, there are countless stories of their willingness to help us.

Wendy had her heart broken as a young woman when her boyfriend Bill, the love of her life, ended their relationship and moved away from the area. Five years later, Wendy was still single because she felt unable to trust after this betrayal. Then Bill's mother called to tell her that he was dying from a brain tumour and only had weeks to live; he wanted to see her and put things right between them. She agonised for days before deciding that she couldn't turn down his last request.

On the way there, she turned back more than once, changing her mind. The third time this happened, she bumped into an elderly lady dressed in black. She hadn't even realised anyone was so close but the lady didn't seem at all annoyed and wasn't hurt. She simply smiled at Wendy and said, "You are loved, and you are doing the right thing."

Stunned, Wendy thanked her and turned away to continue her journey. Then she decided to ask the lady what she meant but, as she looked around, she was astonished to find there was no sign of her; there were no shops she could have gone into and no turnings, yet the elderly lady had vanished in seconds.

Bill and Wendy did make their peace and she supported him until he passed on a few months later. Returning from the funeral, she again met the old lady who was dressed exactly the same as on the previous occasion. This time, she said, "You are loved, and you did the right thing" before again apparently vanishing into thin air.

Wendy is quite sure it was an angel in human form who persuaded her to visit Bill, and then came back to reassure her. Now free from the bitterness of her break-up, she met Iain a few weeks later and they are getting married. She feels that making her peace with Bill allowed her to move on, yet without the encouragement of the angel she might have backed out of the meeting or wouldn't have been so responsive to Iain.[3]

As well as appearing to people in human form, angels are not shy of showing up in all their glory at times. A few years ago, I went for my regular Reiki session with Tina, feeling grumpy and tired. I'd been woken up hearing my name called at 8.15 a.m., which had spoiled my plans for a lie-in, but Ted was still asleep and so was the friend who was staying with us. I couldn't settle again, so by the time I arrived for my appointment later that morning I wasn't very relaxed.

Afterwards, Tina said she'd seen Archangel Raphael, the angel of healing, standing at the foot of the treatment couch. He was so

---

[3]   There are many wonderful stories of angelic beings intervening to help us, appearing in human form or in their winged splendour, in Glynis Amy Allen's prize-winning book *The Angels Beside Us* (Local Legend, 2020).

tall he filled the room, like a pillar of emerald green light, but with a kindly face and huge wings that spread across the room. I had seen that light behind my closed eyelids during the session. As a healer, Tina knew that Raphael worked through her but this was the first time he'd appeared to her in this way and she felt that he was there for me, to let me know I was supported and loved.

When I got home, there were messages on my phone to contact my eldest son. His wife had passed away suddenly that morning, at the exact time I'd heard my name being called. I felt Raphael was there to support me through that time when I needed to be strong for my son and over the next difficult weeks, whenever I felt overwhelmed, I remembered the angelic presence at the Reiki session and immediately felt comforted.

Tina had also seen another lady standing close to Raphael and smiling, and she'd assumed this was a spirit connected to me, also offering support. When I found out about my daughter-in-law's passing, I sent her photo to Tina; yes, it was the same lady she'd seen, so I knew my daughter-in-law wanted me to know she was safe and happy, which was very comforting for all of us at that time.

I believe that angels are everyday channels and connections to the divine as well as supportive friends. A spiritual mentor once told me, "There is no such thing as a small problem – if it's stealing your joy, it's important", and that's why we should never be reluctant to call in the angels. If nothing else, we can be sure they will listen to us without judgement, and a trouble shared is a trouble halved. Indeed, unlike some friends, angels are never too busy for us and it's never too late to call on them for guidance and support. Our guardian angels are around us every day, waiting to help with anything that's bothering us.

An excellent way to build up a rapport with angels is to talk to them every day since, after all, the best friendships are built on communication. Even if we do not immediately feel their presence around us, we can trust that they are there and we can talk to them as friends. We don't need to name names or speak out loud, just put the thought out. At night before we go to sleep, we can thank them for everything that's happened during the day. And when we wake in the morning, we can thank them for the new day and all the blessings to come.

Gratitude always 'raises our vibrations', and being thankful makes it easier to connect with the angels at a level where our energies can align. True gratitude means giving thanks for everything, both good and bad, because even the difficult events can teach us valuable lessons. This is a lifestyle choice. It's impossible to be grateful and negative at the same time, so by focusing on our blessings we automatically shift our energy to a more positive perspective.

For myself, I can say that forming a strong connection with the angels has helped me greatly on my spiritual path, taught me a lot about myself and helped me change for the better. I am more calm and patient, more accepting and forgiving and less judgemental whatever the circumstances. One of the greatest benefits of inviting angelic energy into our lives is learning that the most obvious solution to a problem isn't necessarily the best one: we need to look at the bigger picture and be sure that our choices are for the highest good of everyone concerned. The gentle, loving energy and wise counsel of the angels helps us to do just that.

A Visualisation for Inner Light

Archangel Uriel's name means 'Light of God'. He's responsible for light, truth and inner peace, and it was Uriel who was sent to warn Noah of the impending Great Flood (Genesis 6:13 in the Bible and Surah 11:37 of the Qur'an). Traditionally, he's also thought of as being tasked with giving courage to soldiers going into battle, his red ray and element of fire bringing strength, confidence and determination to those who need it most.

This visualisation can be especially helpful when we are feeling personally overshadowed by fear or despair, or when events in the news such as wars and natural disasters leave us overwhelmed with grief for the troubles of others. We can use it to build our own inner light, since light will always drive away shadow, and to send love, peace and healing to whomever may need it, whether that's family or friends, people who are suffering in other parts of the world or even Mother Earth herself.

* Sit comfortably with closed eyes and ask Archangel Uriel to work with you, to build and to share your inner light. You may visualise him standing before you in ruby red robes or sense his presence; if not, have faith that he is there because you have asked for his help.

* Feel the warmth that emanates from Uriel as he glows with a golden yellow light like the sun on a hot summer day, and feel this radiant light throughout your body; it passes through the skin and travels into your inner being, lighting and warming every single cell. Bask in that light and warmth until you, too, glow like Uriel with beautiful golden yellow light. Feel his warmth in your heart.

✳ Now visualise yourself floating up, rising high above your body and looking down to see your inner light glowing. Know that your light is bright and cannot be extinguished, as you allow it to draw you slowly back into your body.

✳ Ask Archangel Uriel to seal his light inside you by placing a ruby red cloak around your shoulders. It's hooded, with long sleeves that cover your fingertips and it reaches to the floor. You are now fully protected from the shadows by angelic light.

✳ You may wish to send your light out to others in need. Perhaps there's a friend or family member who needs help, or people you've heard about in the news; you may even be thinking of a whole nation or the Earth itself. At first you visualise a dense, dark space in front of you where it's impossible to distinguish any shape or being, yet know there is someone there in that darkness who needs light to bring them out of their shadows.

✳ With hands on heart, feel again the warmth of your inner light and visualise its golden beams reaching out into that dense darkness, its golden rays connecting with the people or places you wish to help. Gradually, their shapes emerge out of the shadows, glowing with Uriel's radiant love and light.

✳ Ask Archangel Uriel to wrap them in a ruby red cloak to seal their own inner light, then say these words, either aloud or mentally: "Archangel Uriel, thank you for sharing your light of wisdom, truth and peace with me and with others, to bring us from the shadows of suffering into the light of joy and love."

✳ Come back slowly to the room, move your fingers and toes a little and have a drink of water. This is a powerful visualisation, so don't rush to do anything else until you have fully settled back into yourself.

CHAPTER NINE

It's in the Cards

My friend Frankie was at a crossroads in her career choices. When she was made redundant, she decided to set up her own business making greetings cards and gifts and also running workshops to teach her skills to others. It was something she'd done as a hobby for years, and she had sold to friends and at various craft fairs. She already had a good stock of materials, built up over many years, so it wouldn't take much investment to step up a gear and turn her hobby into a business.

After about a year, although she was making ends meet she wasn't earning enough to save or to expand her business. Then a friend offered her a hospitality job; it was good money and would leave Frankie with time to add to her stocks, but effectively it would postpone her dream of running craft workshops and ultimately having her own premises, where she could also showcase other crafts and invite people to become partners in her venture. Frankie was already into her fifties and didn't want to delay too much longer.

She decided to ask her favourite Tarot deck whether she should take the job and chose a three-card spread, with the cards representing Yes, No and Likely Outcome in turn.

The Yes card was The Devil. In the Tarot, this is usually seen as representing temptation. In this case, Frankie saw it as the temptation to take the easy way out and settle for paid work but to forego the dream of running her own business and helping others. She was being tempted to take the safe option and focus on the short-term goal of financial security, rather than step out of her comfort zone and pursue the long-term objective of doing something she loved.

The No card was the Eight of Pentacles. The main message of this card is that hard work brings its own reward, encouraging us to keep doing what we're doing because success will come. In Frankie's situation, this card really spoke to her, offering the reassurance she needed to keep working towards her dream. She could afford to play the waiting game a while longer.

The Ace of Wands in the Likely Outcome position convinced Frankie that she should stick with her career path plan and persevere in building her business. This card speaks of new beginnings and a creative pathway. It's encouraging new projects and it hints at future potential. It was all the confirmation Frankie needed to hang on in there and build her business rather than accepting the job offer.

A year later, business had increased considerably and Frankie had been able to save towards her goal of renting business premises and attracting partners to work with her. She has never regretted turning down the job offer.

Some people think that reading cards is something we can only hope to do after years of study to develop our psychic powers and intuitive skills. The good news is, whilst not everyone is drawn to reading cards, it's a skill that many of us can learn with time and patience. As with all spiritual work, intuition also plays a big part in readings; well, that's something we all have our fair share of if we choose to acknowledge and listen to it. Card reading, or cartomancy, is open to us all.

Cards are divination tools, that is to say they can help us connect with the energy around us and, by extension, the higher self, our spirit guides and the angels, in order to answer questions. Other common divination tools are pendulums, runes, crystal balls and tealeaves. Different cultures throughout history have used many weird and wonderful alternatives, from sticks to animal entrails; the important thing is that the method awakens our spiritual intuition.

The sheer range of card decks available nowadays may seem confusing at first but essentially there are Tarot, oracle and angel cards. Each type has its own particular uses, with certain characteristics common to all of them. Below are examples of readings with each type of deck to give an idea of the sort of information we can bring through and how it may help the client. Which type we choose to work with is a matter of personal preference and what resonates most with us; we shouldn't feel we have to work with a particular deck just because someone else has recommended it. And by the way, it's a myth (and probably a marketing ploy) that our first deck of cards should be bought for us!

The Tarot

There are always 78 cards in a Tarot deck: 22 Major Arcana cards and 56 in the Minor Arcana. Major Arcana cards are archetypes with traditional meanings and life and soul lessons, whilst the Minor Arcana is similar in design to regular playing cards with four suits containing cards with numbers up to ten plus the court cards, Page, Knight, King and Queen. If the Major Arcana represent life lessons, people and events, then the Minor Arcana is for the nuts and bolts of day-to-day living. To read the Tarot effectively, we need to become familiar with the traditional meanings and themes of the cards.

Many Tarot decks are based on the original Rider-Waite design of 1910 and generally share common meanings. Yet there are many differently themed decks available, such as Moon Tarot, Witch Tarot and even Disney Villains Tarot! Author and psychic Radleigh Valentine has created a sub-genre called Angel Tarot, where he takes the traditional Tarot and gives it an angelic slant, changing some of the names of the Major Arcana and replacing the traditional suit names of Swords, Cups, Pentacles and Wands with various archangel names or elements. It's Valentine's deck that I use when reading the Tarot.

As the cards are dealt, a story unfolds and each card relates to the others in the spread. Some people feel that there are negative associations with certain individual cards and this makes them wary of readings. However, my belief is that there's no such thing as a bad card reading. Yes, there may be challenges revealed, things that may be hard to hear. But our clients should always feel empowered and optimistic afterwards and we should take care to present everything in positive, encouraging terms.

Tanya's reading stands out for me because of the surprises and reassurances it brought to her. It was in the middle of October and the cards clearly indicated two new babies coming into the family over the coming year. Tanya's daughter was indeed trying for a second child so she wondered whether there could be twins, as nobody else in the family was planning children at that time, but my intuition was that the babies were coming into two families, both strongly linked to Tanya.

With The Empress and the Ace and Page of Raphael (corresponding to Cups in traditional Tarot) all appearing in the spread, it looked like Tanya was about to become a grandma twice over. The Ace and Page cards often speak of new beginnings and, because they were in the same spread as the Empress, I felt these new beginnings were children. Several weeks later, Tanya told me her daughter was indeed pregnant. Then, early in the New Year, she contacted me again to say that her son's partner was also pregnant and the two babies were due within a few weeks of each other.

Now, Tanya and her husband Ray run a successful Internet-based business and, when I saw the Three of Gabriel (corresponding to Wands), I felt expansion was close since the general feeling around this card is of a ship coming in. Tanya was delighted to see it and said that they indeed had plans to develop their business worldwide; when the Emperor card also showed up, this seemed to give the green light. The Emperor is a sign of stability and ambitious plans, also indicating promotion or an upturn in business, and its appearance in the Possible Outcomes position of the spread underlined that Tanya's and Ray's plans were ripe for implementation. The Emperor card can also suggest the need to exercise caution in a business scenario to ensure that one remains in control of the situation; however, paired with the Three of Gabriel it was a card of encouragement.

Before too long, business was very good and Tanya and Ray had no regrets about making their move when they did. They had increased profits without significantly adding to their workload, so they could still spend lots of quality time with their family. Tanya believed that it could have taken them at least another couple of years to get to this stage without the benefit of the insights that had come from the Tarot reading.

Oracle Cards

If Tarot tells an unfolding story, then oracle cards are the self-contained episodes of a series. There is no specific structure to these decks and no traditions of themes or meanings: an oracle deck can contain anything from twelve to a hundred cards or more, based around any theme. Popular ones feature mermaids, dragons, unicorns, the moon, numerology, sacred sites of the world, crystals, animals and more.

These cards are more immediately accessible to people just setting out on their card-reading journey as there is no structure to the decks, so the possibilities for interpretation are unlimited. A client may find it easier to follow the meanings of oracle cards and there's more flexibility for choosing spreads than with Tarot. One may even combine more than one oracle deck in a reading, for example by drawing a card from each of three decks in a three-card reading, or by shuffling two decks together.

On the other hand, the sheer diversity of decks and subject material can be confusing for some people, so it may be best at first to focus on one or two particular decks that seem most interesting. For example, a Chakra deck can be helpful for self-care, pinpointing areas that need working on, whilst a Crystals deck can suggest specific crystals to enhance one's energy state at certain moments. Many people like to have an Affirmation deck to draw from each morning, setting up a positive attitude for the day. There are many ways to use oracle cards other than reading for oneself or others.

Anne had been a widow for less than a year. She was enjoying the independence of living alone but missed having a man around; there was now a potential new suitor in the picture and she felt a reading would help her see things more clearly. She was drawn to the Dragon oracle deck and we used a nine-card spread that is designed to evaluate two choices and help us decide between them. Anne's choices were whether to begin a new relationship with James or spend more time adjusting to her single state.

The first card looks at the present position, and the next three cards examine the first option; the three after these explore the second option and the final two cards refer to the possible outcomes of the two options respectively.

The first card in Anne's reading was Omega Dragon, a sign of beginning again after the ending of a cycle, thus highlighting the choices she was faced with. Alpha Dragon in position two initially seemed to pair well with Omega since one has feminine energy and the other masculine, both having a creative quality. But then the dark blue colour of the Galactic Dragon coming next hinted at a possible block on creative thinking, its shadowy appearance even bringing a note of caution with it. The fourth card, Quan Yin's Pink Dragon, symbolises the need to heal from past relationships and practise self-compassion. There was a mixture of promise and caution in the spread so far, reflecting Anne's state of mind.

The next three cards described well the potential of her alternative choice. Lilac Fire Dragon hints at letting go of things that no longer serve and transmuting negative energy whilst Sunshine Yellow Dragon speaks of bringing joy into our life through connecting more with nature. The Earth and Water Dragon, the last of the three, describes a new phase of life opening up with freedom to create and grow. However, I believe that all cards concerned with nature carry the additional advice to look more deeply into our own nature and discover what we really want from life.

There was such a contrast between the messages of the cards relating to the two options that Anne was already beginning to think it was too soon for her to embark on a new relationship, even though she was attracted to the idea of being part of a couple again. The final two Outcome cards would therefore be important.

The eighth card, for beginning the new relationship, was the Earth and Fire Dragon: clearing is necessary before moving forward. Card nine, for allowing more time, was the Earth and Air Dragon: the recipient needs to be clear about their hopes and dreams for the future. The fact that the final three cards featured the Earth element was not lost on either of us.

However much she missed male company, Anne realised that she still had a lot of inner work to do on grounding and stabilising her energy before embarking on another relationship, and the cards seemed to reinforce this. The overall message of the reading was still very positive, even though it appeared that the cards were stacked against what she wanted, a new relationship. The cards weren't saying No, they were just saying Not Yet.

A year or so later, after remaining friends in the meantime while Anne worked out what she wanted for her future, she and James did become a couple and in due course planned their wedding.

This serves to prove that what's meant for us won't pass us by, and everything happens with divine timing. The reading helped Anne to clarify things and decide on her priorities so she would be in the best possible frame of mind to embark on a new relationship with James. The attraction was already there, but it needed time for the circumstances to be right so that everything could work out well in the end. Neither of them wanted to risk unhappiness by rushing into a relationship before they were ready to be a couple, in a stable and fulfilling relationship with emotional security.

Angel Cards

These are a particular form of oracle card that features Spirit beings which, I believe, imbues them with the special loving and gentle energy that angels are renowned for. Their messages are meant to encourage and empower us and to help with self-knowledge and understanding. In some angel decks we may also find other ethereal beings such as fairies, unicorns and ascended masters represented, and they may be themed around one angel or several, including many you may never have heard of!

The wonderful thing about these cards is that they help to strengthen the connection with the angelic worlds for both the reader and the client. In my experience, an angel card reading has two main aims: to bring confirmation that we are on the right track and to gently guide us in the right direction if necessary. I find that everyone, of whatever religion or none, feels more hopeful and optimistic after these readings because they offer a more personalised experience than any other type of card deck. Even for those who are just becoming familiar with angels, they give a great introduction and encouragement to learn more about these beings of love and compassion.

When I did a reading for Sylvia, the three cards represented her Strength, what she felt in her Heart and what may present a Challenge to her inner calm. Sylvia was at a very low ebb after a series of difficult situations and she was questioning her own judgement and choices. Her self-esteem was low and she needed encouragement to stop her sinking further into negativity.

The Strength card had the message 'Trust your vibes', which gave her a great boost. We talked about how her instincts concerning a particular situation had been proved right but, because a friend had been so vehemently opposed to her perspective, she hadn't acted on it. She had wanted to leave a ladies' group she and the friend belonged to as she felt that some of the members were very judgemental and gossiped about the others. The card reassured her that there was nothing wrong with her intuition. She had only changed her mind because of the pressure put on her so this was no real reflection on her judgement; on the other hand, there was a lesson here, to be more trusting of her own choices and not be swayed when she really felt she was right.

The Heart card was 'The inner voice' and this seemed to underline the message of the first card. Sylvia did believe in the guidance of angels yet didn't believe in her own strengths, so this card reminded her that she was never alone and that angelic help was always there for her. She needed to understand that angelic guidance would never be rushed, nor would it encourage negativity or potential harm to others. An apparently convincing argument isn't always necessarily valid.

Finally, the Challenge card held the message 'Trustworthy friends'. Sylvia laughed out loud at this because she said it was as though all the cards were telling her to trust herself but to be careful around some of her friends. And since a friend had been the main cause of her self-doubt, she felt this last card was inviting her to step away from situations like that.

The colours of the card were predominantly green and yellow, the colours of healing and happiness, encouraging her to make sure she was surrounded by supportive friends so that she may heal her hurts and learn whom to trust. When I saw Sylvia a while later, she seemed much happier and lighter than when she came for her reading; and the friend who caused her to doubt herself so badly is no longer in her immediate circle.

Whichever kind of card deck we choose is a matter of personal preference and depends on what we expect and need from the reading. Tarot cards can cover more aspects of life in a single reading, but clients may not find it easy to be interactive during the reading especially if they don't have much knowledge of how the Tarot works. Oracle card readings can be more user-friendly and creative for both readers and clients, whilst angel cards are excellent when the client is at a low ebb and needs encouragement and inspiration. We always get the reading we need, when we need it most, so we should go with our intuition and enjoy the experience.

As with anything spiritual, there is no right or wrong way to read cards. What works for you is the best way, so be cautious when anyone tries to encourage you in directions you are not comfortable with. Some readers only ever work with the Tarot whilst others prefer oracle cards, and then there are those who happily work with both kinds either separately or together. Don't worry about this; just as clients can never pull 'the wrong cards', if we trust our intuition we will never choose 'the wrong deck'. Indeed, like crystals, it's more likely that the deck will choose us!

At first, it's only natural to feel as though we'll never be able to make sense of card reading. But we must all start somewhere and should not let fear prevent us from doing what we really want to, in any aspect of life. If we are to learn new things, we need to embrace the unfamiliar; and it doesn't seem so strange for long, once we get used to working with our new-found skills.

One of the best ways to introduce ourselves to reading the cards is to choose a deck that we are drawn to and get to know it well before we even try to do a reading. We should look at each card in turn, check out the symbolism and any messages written on it, and ask ourselves what we feel about the card. Does it make us feel happy and optimistic or do we feel there's a hint of caution there? Is it a card that signals the end of a cycle or the beginning of a new phase? But we should not overthink this or spend too long deliberating on each card; if we pick nothing up from it then we set it aside, choose a different card and come back to that one another time.

Once we have worked through the deck, it's time to read the information in the guidebook for each card. More often than not, our own impressions will be mirrored to some extent in the guidebook descriptions because, whether we realise it or not, we've been looking at the cards intuitively. Intuition is something we all have yet often we don't make the most of it, and learning to read cards is one of many ways to connect with our intuition on a regular basis.

When we feel more familiar with our cards, a useful practice is to pull a daily card for ourselves and write down our impressions of what it means for our day. Then see what the guidebook says and compare it with what we've written. At the end of the day, we look back at our morning impressions and consider how the day has played out. This is a great way to get to know the cards and become confident in reading for ourselves. Even if we never progress beyond that stage, we have learned a new skill and can use the cards to become more in tune with what is happening around us, so our self-awareness is bound to improve.

If we feel ready to progress to more in-depth readings, we could start by doing a three-card reading for ourselves or a friend. The guidebook to the deck will have instructions about preparing for a reading; briefly, we need to set an intention for the reading, to give us the information we need to know right now, and ask a question or questions on which to base the reading. Some people like to say a short prayer at this point to bless the deck, asking angels and guides to help us access information for the highest good of everyone concerned. Some will hold the cards over their heart to imprint them with their energy and, if reading for someone else, give the cards to them to draw in their energy as well.

At the outset, it's important to decide what each card in the spread will represent. There will be some model templates in the deck's guidebook or online. Having started with a three-card spread, eventually we find ourselves able to design our own spreads. For example, I tend to use a nine- or ten-card spread when doing private readings because that can uncover quite a lot of information during an hour-long reading.

Debbie was finding it difficult to develop her spiritual connection, feeling that she'd wasted her psychic gifts by ignoring them at a busy period in her life when she hadn't got the time to devote to study. Now that she was making time for Spirit, she didn't feel she was getting anywhere. My own immediate thought was that she was being too hard on herself and, by worrying about it so much, she was keeping her energy low. That never makes for effective communication.

The cards echoed this. The first one she chose had the message 'Take a step back' and this was followed by 'Trust your vibes' and 'Clear your vibes'. At first glance, these may seem confusing, even contradictory.

However, the first card was telling Debbie to relax and be ready to receive, rather than worrying about why she wasn't receiving. The second card was encouraging her to trust her instincts and intuition, whilst the third one was a gentle reminder that she needed to let go of the negative emotions of self-doubt and self-criticism. Further cards also asked her to trust her inner voice and focus her mind on what she wanted, rather than on what she didn't want.

Archangel Chamuel showed up in this spread too, with the message to 'Open your heart' and, as if to underline that, the next card said, 'Love and accept yourself'. These were the two most important cards of all. Archangel Chamuel is the angel of peace and love, and he often shows up when people have difficulty accepting their own choices and respecting themselves. The clear message for Debbie was to stop beating herself up about her perceived failures and to trust in her intuition and be more positive; then her energy would be in flow and she'd be in the best frame of mind for receiving guidance from Spirit.

She felt much more positive after the reading and has since been using meditation to help her relax and clear the chatter from her mind. She's reading a lot, practising her own card spreads, and is learning to congratulate herself on each small success rather that expecting too much too soon. Being much happier in herself, it wasn't long before she was experiencing the connection and communication she'd looked forward to. For Debbie, the angel reading served as confirmation that she would improve her spiritual connections with time and practice, and a reminder that she needed to show herself the same love and kindness she regularly extended to others.

All sorts of elements can contribute to a reading apart from the messages and illustrations on the cards. What are the predominant colours, and are any figures pictured on the cards looking happy or sad, focused or dreamy? Is a card mainly light or dark? What's the setting? How do we feel when we look at it, perhaps sensations of calmness or inner turbulence? If there are numbers associated with it, we may want to check out their spiritual meaning. For example, the number five often signifies change; if the card carries a feeling of dispute, maybe the client or someone around them is having trouble accepting change. All of these subtle meanings can be learned over time and, when we combine our knowledge with our intuitive thoughts, we find we are soon able to give meaningful readings for ourselves or others.

Whilst reading cards is a combination of learned skills and intuition, it's also subjective and largely dependent on who is having the reading and why. The positioning of the cards can also add valuable information to the reading, so we need to look at each reading as an entirely separate event and a new opportunity to learn and grow on our spiritual journey.

Moreover, we should not be too keen to label cards with specific meanings because they can change from one reading to another, particularly with oracle cards. The Tarot may have more layers of meaning and symbolism, but even so there is room for flexibility and we need to approach each reading with a fresh and open mind. The same card can have different meanings depending on its position in the spread and the situation of the client.

Some people like to explore cartomancy and develop their skills privately, but there are also lots of courses and workshops around to help us learn more about the Tarot and oracle cards, either online or in person. Some Mind, Body and Spirit publishers periodically offer free training too. This is usually in conjunction with the release of a new course or book by one of their authors, but no-one is obliged to buy anything so it's a good way to dip our toes in the water of new spiritual practices without having to pay for the privilege. Alternatively, check out what is available locally: New Age and crystal shops will have information on courses and workshops in their area.

When we work with the cards, we are helping our clients to gain insight into what's happening around them, whether the issues they are dealing with are life-altering or apparently minor inconveniences. If something is stealing our joy, it's a challenge that needs to be addressed so that we don't waste any more of our energy on it. The comfort that a reading can offer is a precious gift and it's open to all of us. Each reading is a new adventure and can be full of happy surprises.

CHAPTER TEN

Using Our Energy

Lucy came up to me at a public event and said, "We don't know each other very well but I've been looking at your aura – it's a beautiful arc of purple with red. I sometimes see you in the neighbourhood, from a distance, and it's like you're carrying your personal magical rainbow around with you."

Her comments moved me deeply and left me feeling uplifted. But then, we all carry our own personal rainbows with us in the fields of energy that surround us. I will often see a particular glow around people when I do readings for them, or sometimes when I pass them in the street, although I don't have Lucy's talent for seeing auras in detail.

It is thought that this ability may be a form of synaesthesia, where waves of electrical and chemical activity spreads through the visual cortex of the brain and cause visual symptoms. The functions of the nerves are not harmed in any way by this. But there is also a more spiritual interpretation and there are many who believe that the colours around us can be analysed as signs of our physical, mental and emotional health.

For example, purple is a colour associated with the third eye and crown chakras, and is often seen in the fields of empaths with intuitive and psychic skills. It signifies connection with the universe and non-physical life-forms, and usually indicates creative, questioning thought processes. Red is associated with the root chakra, and bright red in the aura indicates a grounded person who can happily work between the physical and the spiritual worlds and is content in their skin. People with red in their aura don't fear death, which is true of many people with a strong spiritual connection. Orange and yellow in an aura represent self-confidence and joy, whilst green signifies unconditional love and healing energies; pink is nurturing, blue indicates good communication skills and white suggests a divine connection.

Aura reading is actually a skill that can be developed with time and patience – there are courses available – and there's much more to know about patterns, streaks, shades and gaps that all have specific meanings, as well as colour variations to take into consideration.

Yet these comments are just meant to introduce the subject of personal energy in a way we can all identify with. Science has yet to understand all there is to know about energy: just how does telepathy work, and how can atomic particles react to one another instantaneously at vast distances? But these subtle personal energies are an integral component of every one of us. It's important that we find ways to manage and work with our own energies and learn from famous spiritual leaders to identify the energetic characteristics that single them out from the crowd. Indeed, we have a surprising level of autonomy over our personal energy: we can shift it from negative to positive, we can use it to help heal ourselves and others, and we can channel it to manifest what we need to live our best lives.

As we develop our spiritual awareness, to a point where we respond rather than react to events, we begin to create the reality we want rather than being the victims of circumstance. We may not be able to prevent bad things from happening, and there will always be people in our lives who test us sorely, but we can alter the way we perceive challenges and amend the way we navigate through them. In order to do that successfully, we need to understand more about our personal energy and realise that we can invariably use it to our advantage, even in the most difficult of times. This is where our personal power lies.

Martin Luther King Jr. fought a tireless battle for equality and acceptance for everyone regardless of race, gender, beliefs or social standing, and he lost his life because of it. Yet throughout the huge challenges of his life he never lost hope for a better world and he never lost unconditional love for his fellow man. More than fifty years on from his passing, his words still inspire today and they always will. King is memorable not only for his words and actions but for his energy, which came from a place of love. He refused to be drawn into the hatred and bitterness that raged around him. He loved his enemies and forgave them for what they did. It takes a special kind of person to do that.

"Forgiveness is not an occasional act," he said. "It is a permanent attitude."

These words were inspired by a conversation between Jesus and Peter about forgiveness in the Bible. 'Then Peter came to Jesus and asked, "Lord, how many times shall I forgive my brother or sister who sins against me? Seven times?" Then Jesus said, "Not seven times, but seventy times seven."' (Matthew 18: 21, 22) As King pointed out, forgiving somebody multiple times soon becomes a habit.

Many spiritual teachers say that only two energies really matter, fear and love. King encouraged people to live in the energy of love and to spread that love far and wide by loving our enemies and those who do us wrong, because hating them is a lower, fearful energy that allows them power over us.

"I am convinced," he said, "that love is the most durable power in the world. It is not impractical idealism, it's practical realism… To return hate for hate does nothing but intensify the existence of evil in the universe. [We must] cut off the chain of hate and evil, and this can only be done through love."

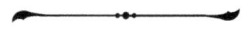

In our bodies, we have four types of energy: physical, emotional, mental and spiritual. Physical energy is the life force that needs to

129

flow freely to keep our bodies healthy and in Chapter 6 we saw how clearing and cleansing our chakras enables the flow of both physical and spiritual energy. (The root, sacral and solar plexus chakras are mainly concerned with the physical, whilst the heart is the bridge that connects them with the essentially spiritual chakras of throat, third eye and crown.) But all four of our bodily energies are inextricably linked and health is not just about the physical, our state of mind is also vital to our wellbeing. Moreover, if we want to connect with the energies of the spirit worlds, we need to give at least as much attention to our emotional, mental and spiritual energies as we do to the physical.

When our mental energy is in a healthy state, we feel happy, strong, empowered and confident; but if our mood is low we are anxious, lacking motivation and confused about ourselves and our situation. We may then make bad decisions or, even worse, allow others to take away our power by making decisions for us. If our emotional energy is out of balance, that's bad news for relationships as we are more likely to get involved in arguments as well as being over-sensitive to criticism or insensitive to the needs of others. Instead of talking out our fears calmly and rationally, we may play the blame game and strike out at those closest to us.

The good news is that our minds are so much stronger than we often realise and we can use that strength to realign our energy whenever we need to. When we do so, we feel more love in our hearts and our relationships improve. We don't make judgements, we don't take things personally and we don't apportion blame, so therefore we don't feel so burdened. We become more accepting of everything and become closer to the unconditional love that is the cornerstone of a spiritual lifestyle.

When spiritual energy is depleted, we lack a sense of purpose and feel overwhelmed, perhaps wondering why we are here at all. What's the point of anything? But if we rebalance that energy, we feel more at peace and less bothered by what's happening around us. We are attending to the needs of the soul and opening up our hearts and minds. Further, strong spiritual energy puts us in the higher state of mind where we can connect with Spirit, using our natural psychic abilities.

It's a wonderful feeling when all four energies are in flow and, although it takes a conscious effort on our part to bring this about, the difference it makes in our lives is absolutely worth it. However, let's be clear about this: managing our energy is not a quick fix, like losing a few pounds so we can slip easily into those special clothes. It's a state of being, a life project if you like. Once we start the work, though, we soon find that it's transformational, and as we get accustomed to managing our energy it gets easier and becomes second nature. The changes shine from us, too, attracting others on the same wavelength and discouraging negative people from latching onto us and draining our hard-won health.

Despite traumas and setbacks, it is possible to reach a state of acceptance where we can be grateful for everything that's happened, good and bad, because these things have made us who we are. We can move to a level where we see the bad times as lessons and stepping stones on our personal journey of growth, so they no longer steal our joy. When we're in this happy, open state, savouring each moment of our lives and grateful just to be in the here and now, we have our personal energy in its healthiest condition.

And when times are hard, we can be strengthened by drawing on the wisdom and inspiration of people like the His Holiness the Dalai Lama. The spiritual leader of Tibet, who refers to himself as "just an ordinary Buddhist monk", is never seen without a smile and a serene expression on his face. In his writings and in the way he lives his life, he demonstrates his understanding of the human condition and his firm belief that we can control and adapt our energy to be happy and at peace with ourselves and our world.

"Anger and hatred are our real enemies," he has said. "Unless we train our minds and work to reduce their negative force, they will continue to disturb us and disrupt our attempts to achieve a calm mind. For the purpose of developing love and compassion, the practice of tolerance is essential, and for that an enemy is indispensable... we should be grateful to them, for they can best help us develop a tranquil mind!"

Now, there's an interesting idea, being grateful for everything that happens and to those who may attack us, because gratitude is valuable in so many ways. He takes this to another level by suggesting that compassion for our enemies – and Tibetans know about this all too well – is an act of strength that means we take on the responsibility of helping protect them from the possible consequences of their actions. Rather than being a sign of weakness it takes real strength because, "Retaliation based on the blind energy of anger seldom hits the target." Keeping calm and choosing our responses based on the energy of love is more productive.

Of course this is not easy, yet we can work with our personal energy by having an honest conversation with ourselves and deliberately focusing our intentions on how we want to shift, on who we want to be. Many people find visualisations or affirmations helpful too, where we're using the power of our minds to connect with the subconscious to bring about changes in our state of being.

What about all those bad past experiences? If we want to be more in the present moment, rather than being tied to the past and replaying traumas that prevent us from moving on and make us feel like victims, we can for example visualise the 'cutting of energetic cords'. This literally enables us to let go of past pain: our conscious mind acknowledges the emotional baggage we need to shift, gives it form and visualises our separation from all the things that no longer serve us yet are holding us back from emotional and spiritual growth. There's a visualisation to help with cutting these cords at the end of this chapter. We don't need to know exactly how this works, only trust that it does, and we will feel lighter and happier afterwards.

Once we have developed our personal energy to the point where we wish to connect with Spirit, we need to rely even more on trust because we simply don't know enough about the energy that makes communication possible. How does the energy of those in Spirit differ from our own? It is often said that spirit energy is pure, unconditional love; well, it's difficult to grasp that someone who never had a good word for anybody while they were on Earth suddenly becomes all peace and love when they transition! What we should remember, though, is that personal energy can change. We have been working to shift our own energy so why shouldn't those in Spirit also be able to do the same? All we can reasonably do is to trust in the guidance and protection of the angels and ensure that we are in a state of being that's as close as we can manage to unconditional love. Then any negative spiritual forces around will not be able to affect us.

This doesn't mean hugging everyone regardless and thinking that everything is wonderful in this world and the next; that's just unrealistic and is not going to move us along our path of learning and growth. What we can and should do, though, is balance our responses to events and people so that we are not permanently riding an emotional rollercoaster, with no sense of inner peace and spiritual wellbeing. And it's all too easy to forget that, as well as words and actions, our thoughts also carry powerful energy. The Law of Attraction tells us that what we focus on becomes our reality, so positive thinking and gratitude bring more blessings into our lives, whilst negative thinking can only lead to negative outcomes. This is what the teachings of spiritual leaders are based upon, and we should seek to learn from them.

Liz took the giant step of moving half of her large family to Spain and buying a business in which they could work together. It needed a great deal of work and Liz and her husband Ralph hadn't realised just how many setbacks there might be. On top of that, Liz began to miss her family acutely; she was at a really low ebb and couldn't see a way to bring her energy back. She wasn't regretting their move, because they were making progress and the family all agreed it would work out well for everyone in the long term. But there were times when she needed to reinforce her belief.

First of all, I took Liz through the Sending Love visualisation in Chapter 3, although with a slight difference. I suggested that she put herself in the centre of the family group and imagine she was looking at a photograph of them all. This proved so powerful for her that her eyes shot open as she felt the force of love enveloping them all. What she was doing here was consciously managing her own energy to connect with the loved ones she was physically separated from and reminding herself why she had chosen to relocate with the family.

Next we talked about gratitude and about seeing each setback as a lesson, therefore turning negative experiences into positive results. From now on, each night Liz would send thanks to the universe for the day, for the good things and the bad; and each time she felt negative about something, she would try to cultivate the habit of switching the energy to gratitude for a lesson learned. Like the seventy-times-seven acts of forgiveness earlier, if we spend enough time doing something it becomes second nature.

Finally, Liz was not to blame herself or other family members when things went wrong, because this achieves nothing. In any case, if everyone is doing their best, where's the blame? We tend to have such high expectations of ourselves that it's more or less guaranteed we'll fall short sometimes; instead, we can learn to congratulate ourselves on each victory, however small, and build ourselves up rather than pulling ourselves down.

A few days later, Liz was looking and feeling much happier. She said that she couldn't believe so much could be achieved with so little real effort. Well, shifting our energy is a big undertaking and if it feels effortless that means we're already on the right path.

We have all experienced the feelings that Liz described, of losing our way, being beset with troubles and not achieving anything. But if we constantly beat ourselves up over perceived failings we make life much harder in all sorts of ways. And if we don't respect ourselves, that's the energy we project to others; it's likely to attract disrespectful people to us who will make us feel even worse. Our thoughts are as powerful, in some cases even more so, than our deeds. It follows that we should focus on positive thought in order to attract positive outcomes into our lives.

The universe responds to our thoughts. Doesn't the universe already know what we need? The problem is that even positive thoughts can get buried under a failure attitude, when we focus too much on our perceived weaknesses and not enough on our strengths. The universe homes in on our focus. If our thoughts are negative, the universe believes these are important to us so we potentially attract more negativity into our lives without even realising it. We're only human and we're bound to get down days when we can't seem to pull ourselves out of a low mood. However, even on the darkest days, it's possible to shift our energy and take the focus away from the negative.

Suppose we are worrying about an upcoming change. Rather than dwelling on its possible negative effects, what we may lose by it, we can try to switch out of our comfort zone and think about the benefits of the change. We all find it difficult at times to accept change but it doesn't just happen randomly. Perhaps we or others close to us have strayed from our soul paths and need to learn a life lesson that can't happen under the present circumstances. So we can try to refocus our thoughts to welcoming the change instead of dreading it by considering at least one benefit of it – and there are bound to be benefits because life is a balance. Once we can identify one good thing about the changes we are facing, we'll come up with more and then it won't seem such a bad thing after all. We may even begin to look forward to change in the future!

Change is a theme that often comes up in psychic readings and, almost without exception, the client doesn't welcome it and it's the main reason they are sitting across the table. Yet once we perceive change as something to be embraced, the energy around the situation lifts and our initial, instinctive resistance fades. Our egos may want us to stay on familiar ground but that's not always the best thing for our souls, is it?

A powerful way to shift our thinking positively is to cultivate an attitude of being grateful for what we have in our lives rather than concentrating on what we prefer to avoid. Not only will gratitude attract more blessings, it's surely energetically impossible to be grateful while simultaneously having negative thoughts. Gratitude is an elevated state of mind; just think how happy and fulfilled we feel when something great happens, like a birth in the family, a successful training course or a move to a new and better home. Now extend that feeling to everything that's good in life, because it's not just the big things that make life worth living, it's the build-up of the small, everyday things that we so often take for granted. And gratitude is like a muscle – the more it's used the stronger its effects become.

We can embrace this way of thinking with a simple daily practice, maybe first thing in the morning or before sleep at night, by consciously acknowledging the good things in our lives and for life itself. Even the worst days have something good about them: a lovely meal, time spent with friends, the beauty of nature around us, in fact anything that uplifts us. We take so much for granted, too, like having a peaceful home with clean water and an electricity supply that so many others lack.

By making a conscious effort to acknowledge these things, gratitude soon becomes second nature. The worries of the mind are calmed down and we are not kept awake at night by niggling thoughts, even after a busy and stressful day. When we view each day as a blessing, we let go of negativity and focus on all that's good.

Once we have learned to shift our perspective in these ways then our physical, emotional, mental and spiritual energy systems will be fully in flow and we can enjoy our best life on every level, aligned with the universe and all it has to offer. Yes, it may take a while before we feel the real benefits coming through, but the truth is that we are much more powerful than we know. We hold autonomy over our own energy and by focusing on it we also surround ourselves with protection so that we feel more confident when dealing with challenging situations or difficult people.

An example of how our energy works for us, sometimes even without our realising it, was when Terri approached me for a reading at a public event. I could tell from her body language that she was reluctant, yet some invisible force was bringing her to me and wasn't going to let go. She began by saying that she didn't believe in the afterlife or angels and didn't think I could do anything to help her… but she just felt she needed to speak to me.

I reassured her that I didn't promise to bring messages through from the spirit world and didn't make predictions for the future, just that spiritual energy works through psychics to bring information that's needed – and not necessarily what the client wants to hear. Having agreed the ground rules, I took out my angel cards for their gentle, uplifting energy, and Terri made her choice. It was clear from the start that she was undergoing significant changes and wasn't at all happy about them.

"Yes," she said, "but that could be true for anyone. Tell me something specific, then I might have something to believe in."

It was already clear that a simple card reading wasn't going to achieve anything for Terri, other than creating even more mental barriers. Spiritual intuition kicked in now and I could tell that a very close family member had hurt her so badly that she couldn't let go of the pain; she even felt her life no longer worth living because others were siding with this person against her. She needed to release this energy, accept the situation and look at it in another way rather than wishing things were different and assuming the blame.

Terri broke down in tears at this point, apologised for "being weak" and agreed that my intuition was correct. Moreover, she felt she could have done more to sort things out and avoid the situation. I handed her the tissues and waited until she felt able to continue, saying it was good that she was beginning to release her stress and she should cry when she needed to rather than putting on a brave face.

The trouble is, when we put up protective barriers, physical or emotional, they keep out the good stuff as well as the bad so that we can neither give nor receive the love we all deserve. One of the reasons for Terri feeling that everyone was against her was because she was casting herself as the villain: the energy we project is the energy we attract to ourselves. If we want others to respect our choices, we must first respect ourselves and trust in our own intuition and judgement. Choices and decisions are seldom unilateral because others with their own visions of reality are involved; it's rarely the case that one is wrong and the other is right. We can only be responsible for our own thoughts and actions and, if we act in good faith and with the best intentions for all involved, that's all we can do.

So Terri needed to stop berating herself for the situation she found herself in, accept what had happened and work out the way forward rather than trying to turn back the clock. I now sensed a softening in her attitude and she seemed more relaxed in her chair, so I suggested that we go through the Sending Love visualisation (as with Liz, earlier). At first she had difficulty with it, not surprisingly, but gradually she was able to direct her energy to her family members. Afterwards, she was smiling and said she felt calmer and happier than she had in months, and thanked me for what I'd done.

But of course, I explained, I hadn't done anything. She had achieved her relaxed state by managing her own energy and steering her thoughts towards love, acceptance and moving forward. Yes, I had helped by picking up on her state of mind as she arrived and using my spiritual intuition to identify her situation. Yet it was her own unconscious energy that had known what was needed and had drawn her to me, even though she had no idea why and didn't believe in what I seemed to be offering...

All our lives will be so much better when we learn how to tune in to our own inner energy, and that of others, and listen to what it has to tell us. Everything we think, say and do every day is governed by this energy, as is all psychic and spiritual work; it helps us to navigate our lives, to meet our challenges, to accept and let go and move forward.

This is where our real power lies and it's never too late to step into it. Welcome to the Soul Cave!

A Visualisation for Cutting Energetic Cords

Archangel Michael is the angel of protection and justice, and one of his functions is to help us cut the energetic cords that bind us to people and situations in the past. Everything we think and do leaves trails of energy that keep us attached to whatever happens in our lives. Some of these attachments are welcome whilst others are not as they prevent us from moving on from anything that no longer serves us.

This visualisation can help us detach from anything that may be keeping us anchored in the past; it will leave us feeling lighter and happier as we are effectively parcelling up the negative influences in our lives and separating ourselves from them. This helps us see things with a clearer perspective, a vital part of processing hurt, healing and moving on. We can use this visualisation whenever we find impressions from the past intruding and stealing our joy in the present moment.

* Make sure you won't be disturbed for a while and then get comfortable in a chair or lying down, with eyes closed. You should be completely relaxed before you begin.

* Now visualise a ball of black modelling clay in your hands. It may be quite small but, as you roll it around, see yourself adding layers by transferring all your concerns about past hurtful situations and people to the ball so that it grows larger. When everything that's worrying you has been added to the ball, add a final layer of the subconscious worries and triggers that may be buried deep in the mind.

✳ Attach a string to the ball. It doesn't matter how long or short it is, or what it's made from, just know the string is there. See yourself holding the end of the string between thumb and forefinger, with the ball containing everything that no longer serves you cupped in the palm of your hand. Fling that ball away as hard and as far as you can, and watch it go out of sight.

✳ Because you are still attached to the ball via the string, it will come bouncing back towards you very fast. But don't worry, this is all part of the process and it's not going to hit you.

✳ Now call on Archangel Michael to step forward with his sword of light and cut through the energetic cords represented by the string in your hand. Watch the sword swing down powerfully and slice through the cords with one blow. The black ball is now flying away out of sight. It has no power over you now and it isn't coming back.

✳ Thank Archangel Michael for his help. You may feel a comforting presence, like a hug around your shoulders, but just trust that he is there because you called on him for help.

✳ When you feel ready, bring yourself back to the here and now and open your eyes, move your limbs a little and take a drink of water. Take a little time to reflect on your visualisation while it's all fresh in the mind, and know that pain of the past can no longer bring you down.

CHAPTER ELEVEN

Inhabiting the Soul Cave

The Soul Cave has described various ideas, strategies and philosophies to help us navigate our challenges and come through them feeling stronger, more empowered and in a better place energetically. We've looked at tools that can help on our journey of discovery, such as crystals and oracle cards, and explored how to expand our consciousness to enable us to take the next step of communication with the spirit world. There has also been the comfort and inspiration of real-life stories and the teachings of spiritual leaders past and present.

Now it's up to each one of us to work on our own energy, to step into our power and transform our life for the better – nobody can do that for us! But once we start managing our energy with purpose and commitment we will soon see improvements in every aspect of life. This is an ongoing project, a new state of being and not a temporary fix, and we must each experiment to find the best way to inhabit our own particular Soul Cave. What works for one may not resonate with another and each particular soul's needs are very different to others', as are the everyday challenges we have to deal with. With time, though, inhabiting our Soul Cave becomes second nature.

Let's not pretend that this is easy or that life will immediately be all sweetness and light. But when we are fully able to tune into our own energy, we resolve to deal with whatever is stealing our joy instead of pushing it beneath the surface and allowing it to build into something bigger. We work to turn things around, we acknowledge what is bothering us, then find something that brings us joy to counterbalance any feelings of anxiety or sadness. We thank the universe for our blessings, great or small, and also give thanks for whatever challenges us, because there is benefit in everything we experience: good or bad, all these things are guiding us on our spiritual journey.

Cultivating an attitude of gratitude, including learning to be thankful for our challenges, may be one of the most important of all steps on the spiritual path. We can probably all remember many of the mistakes we have made; that's because we learned something new. Indeed, we learn best when we are outside our comfort zone and dealing with unfamiliar situations. Once we are safely through, hopefully we remember what we learned and make use of it moving forward. So when life challenges us, we must ask ourselves what we can learn from this and be grateful for the opportunity. With a change of attitude, life improves greatly.

Stepping into our power means starting to look for a new way of being. Only when we detach from dramas and focus solely on our own state of mind can healing happen. When the mind is confused or constantly in motion, we have neither the presence nor the emotional space to see situations clearly; we come from a place of fear and are likely to react in a knee-jerk way, which only makes things even more difficult to handle. Our resolve must be to respond in a spiritual way.

The single best thing we can do for ourselves is learning to shift our energy. It may seem difficult at first yet in a surprisingly short time it becomes normal. So instead of wondering, 'Why is this happening to me?' we ask, 'What can I learn from this?' We step out of victim mode and set the intention to learn and to grow from every situation, the first and most vital step. Once we decide to manage our responses, rather than perhaps merely limit the collateral damage, we are abandoning feelings of fear and moving into the energy of love that opens the door to all sorts of possibilities.

When we are kind, both to ourselves and to others, we feel happier because it feels good to give and receive kindness and compassion. It's the same when we experience joy, when we laugh or spend time with people who nourish our minds and spirits. Conversely, when we are unhappy or deliberately unkind to someone else for whatever reason, we bring our energy low. We must be determined to focus on holding our energy high and, when it slips, shifting it as soon as possible using some of the strategies described here.

When we are no longer living in fear, of change or new responsibilities or others' attitudes, we surprise ourselves with what we can achieve. And when we shift into the energy of love and trust, everything shifts.

Loving and trusting ourselves is at the core of everything. Do we question our own abilities and choices, assume we are responsible for perceived failings? Is someone else blaming us? In these ways, our self-belief diminishes and this is an unhealthy mindset to carry through life. We can break this cycle by simply reminding ourselves that we are not responsible for everything that happens and nor can we be expected to deal with every situation life throws at us; we are just one element of the situation, interacting with other people and events. Other people's choices and perceptions need be no concern of ours, they are responsible for themselves. And just as we would not try to bend others' will to suit ourselves, they cannot be allowed to do the same to us.

Alongside gratitude, an attitude of acceptance – especially of those things we cannot change – is important if we are to avoid conflict and make life better for ourselves and those we love. Yes, we should make our wishes and expectations clear, but everyone has free will and their own ideas, based on previous experiences and conditioning. Despite our best efforts, things won't always work out the way we expect or would like them to. That's the way life is.

There's another aspect to this, too. When things don't play out as we wish, it doesn't mean we did anything wrong; it may just not be 'the right time'. Those things that are in alignment with our soul's journey, things that we need, will not pass us by and there will always be another opportunity when the timing for creating our new reality is right. So if the dream job doesn't materialise, or we're outbid for the house we wanted, it's nobody's fault and it's not because our lucky shirt was in the wash; it's because this is not what we need right now. Just as the lessons we need to learn will present themselves again and again until we accept them, so the right opportunities will return.

Accepting reality and waiting patiently are no reflection on our abilities or choices, and there is no reason to blame ourselves or anyone else when things don't play out as hoped or expected. We should simply continue to make our decisions with integrity and from a position of love. All we can do is our best and that will always be good enough because humans are not blessed with superpowers. Acknowledging that, we move into the energy of acceptance and life becomes so much easier and happier.

Further, true acceptance only comes when we exercise true forgiveness, when we are able to let go of the past along with the energetic cords that keep us tethered to it. Brooding on the past steals our joy in the present moment and, moreover, prevents us from accepting responsibility for our own actions. Whoever may have been ostensibly to blame for a situation, once it's played out it's done, and holding on to fear and anger from that time serves no good purpose. Blaming our perceived failure to live the life we aspire to on past events, others' roles in them or our own imagined weaknesses, is disrespectful to ourselves and only keeps our energy low. Replaying feelings of bitterness, despair or regret is certainly not good for our mental health, either.

Moving on may not always be easy, but it is hugely empowering and more conducive to our future happiness. Spiritual wellbeing depends on being content in the moment and grateful for life as it is, neither tied to the past nor fearful of the future. When we are grateful for what we have, accepting of what we cannot change and free of regret and blame, we naturally attract more blessings into our lives. As a result, our state of mind improves, raising our mental, emotional and spiritual energy to a level where we can experience profound happiness and joy in the moment.

> The cornerstones of a happy and spiritual life are love,
> gratitude, acceptance and forgiveness.

Happiness is our personal energy. It is not something that we can acquire. We take it with us wherever we go. If we are not happy now, we won't achieve happiness by moving to a bigger house, finding a different job or winning the lottery. It doesn't depend on the absence or presence of particular people or things because it's a state of mind, not a destination. When we learn to manage our energy, look after our own self-care and have a loving attitude, including towards those things and people that challenge us, we can be happy right now.

"The purpose of life," said the Dalai Lama, "is to be happy, and the key to happiness is peace of mind. This is not something that can be bought, inner peace has to be cultivated by each of us from within."

So we need to be the gardeners of our happiness, not the pursuers, and it's something to work on for our souls' satisfaction and for holistic health in mind, body and spirit. It's important to identify things that may be compromising our happiness and to find ways to deal with them, making sure there are boundaries in place to protect our energy. We shouldn't feel bad about saying "No", indeed it can be incredibly empowering provided we practise kindness when we turn people down. It's easy to be dragged down by guilt in such circumstances. But if we continually set aside our own needs to accommodate other people, two things are likely to happen: we will deplete our physical energy and we will start to resent always being on call, so our emotional energy will be compromised as well. This in turn has a knock-on effect on our mental and spiritual energy, leaving us feeling overwhelmed.

There must be balance in all things, and there will be times when we need to focus on our own self-care. This is not indulgence and it's certainly not selfish or self-centred, it's a wise investment in our holistic health and our future happiness. And self-care helps us to connect with ourselves and with others at a much deeper level. Identifying our own needs encourages a sense of purpose, and we realise that life isn't just a trial of our patience and resources but a journey of discovery where we learn about ourselves and the world around us. In this way, we can work towards a genuine sense of peace and inner calm. Then, when our personal energy is in flow, we are in the best state of mind to manifest what we want in our lives.

There's always a chance that our new-found flow and sense of purpose may be too much for some people around us, those who resist change and recognise that we are becoming 'different'. That shouldn't be allowed to compromise our inner happiness or hold us back from creating the reality we want. The phrase "It is what it is" sends out a signal that we are content with whatever happens, we accept that some situations will not work out as we or others may like, and we can't be manipulated by others.

Living spiritually has little to do with organised religion. It means being at one with nature, which includes our own nature as much as the beauty around us. It means connecting deeply with our souls to learn what we really need, and then making sure we address those needs whilst always showing empathy and understanding for those around us. We cannot know what others have been through to make them what they are, any more than they can know about the challenges we have faced and overcome.

The spiritual way means acting with kindness, to others as much as to ourselves. If others feel threatened by our sense of self and our commitment to a new way of being, it would of course be commendable to consider their feelings. But we should not be distracted from our path because, when we are happy and fulfilled, all our relationships will benefit. Moreover, we serve as role models to others, showing them that it's possible to be self-reliant and to take charge of life yet still be kind and compassionate.

We can manifest a happy, peaceful and fulfilled life by being confident that we can achieve anything we set our minds to, with the patience to wait for the right time to realise our dreams and goals. We do this by getting to know ourselves at a soul level, and by learning to focus our energy with determination on the spiritual path. It's not going to happen overnight, but when we truly believe in ourselves and step boldly into our personal power, we embrace what our soul needs rather than settling for a life less lived.

It is never too late to step into our power and create our best life, whatever challenges we may need to navigate along the way. Now is always the right time to explore our own Soul Cave and build a sacred space where we will always feel happy and fulfilled.

Postscript

All our yesterdays have gone
and the future isn't here
but when we wish our lives away
we always live in fear

This moment is all that matters
it's a gift for every soul
let's not replay past hurt and pain
but move on and be whole

Let's celebrate life's blessing
and all its challenge too
helping us to learn and grow
and live a life that's new

Our purpose is to learn to love
to accept and to forgive
with gratitude for all that is
and in this moment live

If you have enjoyed this book...

Local Legend is committed to publishing the very best spiritual writing, both fiction and non-fiction. You may also enjoy:

LOVE, DEATH AND BEYOND
Helen Ellwood (ISBN 978-1-910027-51-6)

Helen had always been almost afraid of living, believing that mere dark oblivion awaited her in the end. Trained in medical sciences and having rejected religious beliefs, she often felt terrified. But Beryl the hamster changed everything when her soul rose from her body at death, and Helen was shocked into opening herself to the spiritual and the numinous. The paranormal experiences came one after another now and it was soon clear that the human mind was far more powerful, and consciousness far more enduring, than she had imagined. Every reader will identify with the author's doubts and fears, and be inspired by this beautifully written memoir.

Winner of the national *Spiritual Writing Competition* and Bronze Medal in *The Wishing Shelf Book Awards*

"...compelling... intriguing..." with score 94%

PAST LIFE HEALING
Judy Sharp (ISBN 978-1-910027-52-3)

Do we live many lives, and could trauma of the past still be affecting our health and wellbeing here and now? The author was completely healed of her own severe claustrophobia in one session and now has decades of professional experience helping others with issues from fear of flying to stubborn weight gain. This truly eye-opening book gives many evidential case studies here, alongside a wealth of information about the concept of past lives across history and different cultures, as well as details of the extensive research carried out in this field.

Winner of the national *Spiritual Writing Competition*.
"A fascinating insight… highly recommended!"

The Wishing Shelf Book Awards

GHOSTS OF THE NHS
Glynis Amy Allen (ISBN 978-1-910027-34-9)

It is rare to find an account of interaction with the spirit world that is so wonderfully down-to-earth! The author simply gives us one extraordinary true story after another, as entertaining as they are evidential. Glynis, an hereditary medium, worked for thirty years as a senior hospital nurse in the National Health Service, mostly in A&E wards. Almost on a daily basis, she would see patients' souls leave their bodies escorted by spirit relatives or find herself working alongside spirit doctors – not to mention the Grey Lady, a frequent ethereal visitor! A unique contribution to our understanding of life, this book was an immediate bestseller.

Winner of the Silver Medal in the
national *Wishing Shelf Book Awards*.

"What a fascinating read. The author has a way of putting across a story that is compelling and honest… highly recommended!"

THE QUIRKY MEDIUM
Alison Wynne-Ryder (ISBN 978-1-907203-47-3)

Alison is the co-host of the TV show *Rescue Mediums*, in which she puts herself in real danger to free homes of lost and often malicious spirits. Yet she is a most reluctant medium, afraid of ghosts! This is her amazing and often very funny autobiography, taking us back stage of the television production as well as describing how she came to discover the psychic gifts that have brought her an international following.

Winner of the Silver Medal in the
national *Wishing Shelf Book Awards*.

"Almost impossible to put down."

AURA CHILD
A I Kaymen (ISBN 978-1-907203-71-8)

One of the most astonishing books ever written, telling the true story of a genuine Indigo child. Genevieve grew up in a normal London family but from an early age realised that she had very special spiritual and psychic gifts. She saw the energy fields around living things, read people's thoughts and even found herself slipping through time and able to converse with the spirits of those who had lived in her neighbourhood. This is an uplifting and inspiring book for what it tells us about the nature of our minds.

5P1R1T R3V3L4T10N5
Nigel Peace (ISBN 978-1-907203-14-5)

With descriptions of more than a hundred proven prophetic dreams and many more everyday synchronicities, the author shows us that, without doubt, we can know the future and that everyone can receive genuine spiritual guidance for our lives' challenges. World-renowned biologist Dr Rupert Sheldrake has endorsed this book as "...vivid and fascinating... pioneering research..."

A national runner-up in
The People's Book Prize awards.

A MESSAGE FROM SOURCE
Grace Gabriella Puskas (ISBN 978-1-910027-00-4)

Beautiful and inspiring poetry of the Spirit that reaches deep within the consciousness, awakening the reader to higher states of awareness, spiritual connection and love. The author, in familiar and thoughtful language, explores the power of meditation, the nature of the universe and of time, our place within the environment and who we truly are as creative beings of light and sound.

Winner of the national
Spiritual Writing Competition.

TAP ONCE FOR YES
Jacquie Parton (ISBN 978-1-907203-62-6)

This extraordinary book offers powerful evidence of human survival after death. When Jacquie's son Andrew suddenly committed suicide, she was devastated. But she was determined to find out whether his spirit lived on, and began to receive incredible yet undeniable messages from him on her mobile phone... Several others also then described deliberate attempts at spirit contact. This is a story of astonishing love and courage, as Jacquie fought her own grief and others' doubts in order to prove to the world that her son still lives.

"A compelling read."
The national Wishing Shelf Book Awards.

DAY TRIPS TO HEAVEN
T J Hobbs (ISBN 978-1-907203-99-2)

The author's debut novel is a brilliant description of life in the spiritual worlds and of the guidance available to all of us on Earth as we struggle to be the best we can. Ethan is learning to be a spirit guide but having a hard time of it, with too many questions and too much self-doubt. But he has potential, so is given a special dispensation to bring a few deserving souls for a preview of the afterlife, to help them with crucial decisions they have to make in their lives. The book is full of gentle humour, compassion and spiritual knowledge, and it asks important questions of us all.

ODD DAYS OF HEAVEN
Sandra Bray (ISBN 978-1-910027-17-2)

If you feel that you've lost the joy in your life and are not sure where you're going, this book is written for you. Sandra knows those feelings all too well. Rocked by mid-life events, she refused to be a victim of circumstances and instead resolved to treat them as opportunities for change and growth. She looked for a spiritual 'guide book' to offer her new thoughts and activities for each day, but couldn't find one – so she wrote it! In this book, and her sequel *Even More Days of Heaven*, we find almost four hundred brilliantly researched suggestions, sure to life our spirits.

> Runner-up in the national
> *Spiritual Writing Competition*.

Local Legend titles are available as paperbacks and eBooks. Further details and extracts of these and many other beautiful books for the Mind, Body and Spirit may be seen at

https://local-legend.co.uk

Ingram Content Group UK Ltd.
Milton Keynes UK
UKHW020630090523
421456UK00016B/430

9 781910 027578